EXPRESSIVE ARTS IN THE PRIMARY SCHOOL

∎

EDITED BY
JUDITH PIOTROWSKI

SPECIAL IN ORDINARY SCHOOLS NEEDS

SPECIAL NEEDS IN ORDINARY SCHOOLS
General editor: Peter Mittler

Associate editors: Mel Ainscow, Brahm Norwich, Peter Pumfrey,
Rosemary Webb and Sheila Wolfendale

Expressive Arts in the Primary School

Titles in the Special Needs in Ordinary Schools series

Meeting Special Needs in Ordinary Schools: An Overview (2nd edition)

Assessing Special Educational Needs
Management for Special Needs
Reappraising Special Needs Education

Concerning pre- and primary schooling:

Primary Schools and Special Needs: Policy, Planning and Provision (2nd edition)
Pre-School Provision for Children with Special Needs
Expressive Arts in the Primary School
Improving Children's Reading in the Junior School

Concerning secondary schooling:

Secondary Schools for All? Strategies for Special Needs (2nd edition)
Further Opportunities: Learning Difficulties and Disabilities in Further Education
Responding to Adolescent Needs: A Pastoral Care Approach
Secondary Mathematics and Special Educational Needs
Shut Up! Communication in the Secondary School

Concerning specific difficulties:

Children with Hearing Difficulties
Children with Learning Difficulties
Children with Speech and Language Difficulties
Educating the Able
Improving Classroom Behaviour: New Directions for Teachers and Pupils
Mobility for Special Needs
Working with Parents of Children with Special Needs

Forthcoming:

Spelling

Expressive Arts in the Primary School

Edited by Judith Piotrowski

CASSELL

AE-1B

(OL2OO)

Cassell
Wellington House
125 Strand
London WC2R 0BB

215 Park Avenue South
New York
NY 10003

First published 1996

British Library Cataloguing-in-Publication Data
A catalogue record for this book is available from the British Library.

ISBN 0-304-33418-9 (hardback)
      0-304-33419-7 (paperback)

Typeset by Textype
Printed and bound in Great Britain by Biddles Limited, Guildford and Kings Lynn

Contents

Editorial foreword

The expressive arts should have a central place in the experiences offered by any school to children who may be experiencing difficulties or obstacles in other areas of the curriculum. They allow pupils to explore creative and aesthetic dimensions of experience and to express feelings and emotions in ways which can enhance self-esteem and a sense of achievement.

The publication of the first edition of this book took place just before the introduction of the National Curriculum. Right from the start, teachers and parents insisted that all children with special educational needs must be fully included in the National Curriculum and were as entitled as all other childen to a 'broad and balanced curriculum which met their individual needs' (Department for Education and Science, *Policy to Practice*, 1989).

The current revision of the National Curriculum has tried to ensure that children with special educational needs were taken into account from the beginning rather than as an afterthought. For all subjects, there is a common requirement to make appropriate provision for pupils who need to use:

- means of communication other than speech, including computers, technological aids, signing, symbols or lip reading
- non-sighted methods of reading such as Braille, or non-visual or non-aural ways of acquiring information
- technological aids in practical and written work
- aids or adapted equipment to allow access to practical activities within school and beyond

Helpful as this may be, thought also needs to be given to the far greater number of pupils with special educational needs who do not have a sensory or physical impairment but who do have difficulties in learning. The origin of such difficulties may lie not so much in the pupil but in the requirements of the curriculum.

Despite the substantial and overdue modifications to the requirements of the National Curriculum, there is a risk that the current emphasis on the raising of standards in the core subjects may result in less time for non-core subjects. Art, music and dance, not to mention the other activities discussed in this book, may suffer as a result.

The introductory chapter to the first edition of this book, *Encouraging Expression* (1988), by the late Tessa Roberts and to the revised edition by Judith Piotrowski have reaffirmed the place of the expressive arts in the revised curriculum and richly demonstrated how this can truly be a curriculum for all.

Professor Peter Mittler
University of Manchester
September 1995

The contributors

Judith Piotrowski is a lecturer in education at the University of Manchester responsible for the art course within the primary PGCE. She also lectures on the English course, an Advanced Diploma in Specific Learning Difficulties (Dyslexia), and runs MEd modules in art and specific learning difficulties. She has a background in teaching at all levels of the primary school and is currently working on her Ph D examining integration and responsibility for learning in mainstream primary schools.

Andy Jones has worked as an actor and as a teacher of drama and dance within a comprehensive school. He is now a lecturer in drama-in-education at Manchester Metropolitan University, where he is the co-ordinator of the PGCE Expressive Arts course as well as a lecturer on the IMSET Modular Programme.

Gill Payne has worked in a variety of primary secondary schools and was for 25 years a lecturer in the Drama Department, Didsbury School of Education, Manchester Metropolitan University. She is now Senior Lecturer in Speech and Drama, Rose Bruford College.

John Rainer is Subject Leader for Drama at Didsbury School of Education, Manchester Metropolitan University. He worked in Theatre-in-Education and taught in a Bradford inner-urban multicultural comprehensive community school before becoming an advisory teacher for drama in Wigan. He is a founder member of National Drama and has been a Youth Theatre director for the last 15 years.

Dr Rita Ray is a qualified teacher with great expertise across the curriculum, specifically in English, maths, art, geography and assessment. Rita has taught across the primary age range in both mainstream and special education. When not working in the Centre for Primary Education at the University of Manchester, she writes books for children.

Patricia Sanderson has taught in various schools and colleges in the UK and the USA and at present lectures in the Education Department of Manchester University. She has published a wide range of book chapters and articles on physical education and dance, and is currently a member of the curriculum committee of the Physical Education Association, the Editorial Advisory Group of the *British Journal of Physical Education Research Supplement*, and the Editorial Board of the *European Physical Education Review*.

Anthony Walker taught music in a wide range of schools for 19 years prior to working in teacher training at De La Salle College of Higher Education, Manchester. He is now Honorary Tutor in Education at the University of Manchester, where he has led courses in primary music for those training to teach the hearing impaired. He was recently awarded a doctorate for his research in music education and has written and co-written several books on music and children.

Acknowledgements

I wish to express my thanks to all the contributors to this book who have produced excellent chapters well within time limits. I am grateful to Elizabeth Moore and Joanne West, both of whom were students of mine, for the use of their teaching practice experiences in the two case studies presented in Chapter 1. Particular thanks go to my family for their support.

I also wish to thank the following for permission to reprint copyright material:

Gareth Owens, 'Miss Creedle teaches creative writing', from *Song of the City*, published by HarperCollins Publishers Ltd. Reprinted by permission of the publisher.

Liz Lochhead, 'Kidspoem/Bairnsong', from *Penguin ModernPoets*, volume 4, published by Penguin. Reprinted by permission of the author.

Introduction

The Arts are in a peculiarly vulnerable position within the framework of the National Curriculum. The context of the publication of the NC Statutory Orders for Arts Disciplines demonstrates this. The publication of Art and Music in the final round along with Dance, tucked away in the PE document, neatly placed key areas of the arts in the bottom tier of a three-tier structure. The areas of drama, oracy and creative writing have been included in the English document. Placing significant arts disciplines in a core document is a mixed blessing; on the one hand they are part of a core subject usually managed by a senior member of staff with some status, and on the other hand they are at once subject to the various and competing demands for resources and time for the teaching of reading.

At the same time as the statutory orders were being published, and revised, there was the on-going debate taking place about initial teacher training and the move towards training different types of teachers and instructors for the primary years. These suggested routes have included the training of teachers' assistants for Key Stage 1 (Hugill, 1993) who would have particular expertise in the teaching of literacy and numeracy skills. The six-subject BEd was proposed in 1992 by O'Hear, the six subjects, typically, being taken from those suggested by the Centre for Policy Studies: English, mathematics, RE, 'a scientifically orientated subject', history, geography and perhaps a foreign language (Lawlor, 1992). The arts are conspicuous by their absence in the proposed new routes. Exceptionally, Wragg (1992) gives particular emphasis to the arts as forming a key area of learning when he outlined his proposals for a Key Stage 1 curriculum: 'Go for literacy supported by four other major fields.' The other areas being: numeracy, the arts, the world around us (humanities), and how the world works (including science and technology) (Hofkins, 1992). Wragg's view that the arts would form a central part of the primary curriculum is indeed the exception rather than the norm.

The message is clearly that the arts are seen as largely peripheral to the essential business of the curriculum. To return to my opening comment that the arts are in a peculiarly vulnerable position, the arts are there in the orders but it will still require the commitment of energetic teachers and arts co-ordinators to fulfil the potential contribution of the arts to the education of all children in primary schools.

The above commentary regarding the context of the arts in the National Curriculum does not, however, reflect the commitment to the arts in primary schools themselves. In the typical primary school there is usually an abundance of evidence of the celebration of children's achievements within the arts. There exists the desire for the arts to demonstrate the extent of attainment by pupils within a particular school. Achievement in the arts are so often the hallmark of the quality of education on offer in a school.

The specific focus of this book is a consideration of the role of and apporaches to teaching and learning in the arts for primary school children with special needs. The authors of this book uphold the stated intentions of the National Curriculum of breadth, balance and universality. In each chapter the authors present the relevant issues affecting their particular discipline and detail appropriate responses. I have been most fortunate to have been able to gather together such a team of experts all of whom have written with great insight, knowledge and sensitivity.

A major recurrent theme throughout the book is the value of arts education in the education of all children. Experience within the arts is of additional not exclusive value to children with special needs. The following is a quote from Tessa Roberts' book, *Encouraging Expression: Arts in the Primary Curriculum* (1988). It is both a useful summary of the purpose of this text and a sincere acknowledgement of her contribution to the field of primary education. In her writing she

> examined those areas that draw most essentially on the human propensity to create, to express and to appreciate. These are the kind of experiences offered by the arts and they are regarded as so vital to the development of the child that it is considered legitimate to isolate them. A curriculum that neglects opportunities for creation, expression and appreciation would be a sterile curriculum needed. This would be true for any child but it is particularly so for children whose special needs may render the liberating and enriching effects of experiences in the arts more necessary, or make success in other areas of the curriculum more difficult to achieve.
>
> (p.1)

In 1989 the Calouste Gulbenkian Foundation referred to 'the cycle of constraint' which exists in the development of the arts in primary schools due to the lack of teachers with appropriate training in the arts. Teachers in primary schools will need all their undoubted enthusiasm for the arts to ensure that the context of the arts within the NC doesn't create a 'cycle of restrain' for *any* of their pupils.

REFERENCES

Calouste Gulbenkian Foundation (1989) *The Arts in the Primary School.* London.

Hugill, B. (1993) Nursery teaching reforms call up a Mums' Army. *Observer,* 9 May 1993.

Lawlor, S. in Hofkins, D. (1992) Nine piece jigsaw goes up in the air. *Times Educational Supplement,* 2 October 1992.

O'Hear, A. in Pyke N. (1992) Ministers fuel fear of training overhaul. *Times Educational Supplement,* 2 October 1992.

Roberts, T. (ed.) (1992) *Encouraging Expression: Arts in the Primary School.* London: Cassell.

Wragg, T. in Hofkins, D. (1992) Nine piece jigsaw goes up in the air. *Times Educational Supplement,* 2 October 1992.

Art for all, almost

Judith Piotrowski

> Art is a means of communication not bound by written or spoken language and enables pupils with special needs of all kinds to develop a capacity for self-expression. Art can help to develop positive attitudes in pupils, not only to themselves but also to other people. As with any other pupil, the teacher's task is to help the pupil with SEN to experience success and satisfaction in art.
>
> (NCC, 1992, F2, para. 5.1)

The 1978 Warnock Report, the subsequent 1981 Education Act and the 1988 Education Reform Act established, among many significant innovations, the legal framework for the education of all children between the ages of 5 and 16 years. That education was to be broad, balanced and universal, i.e. for all. The publication of the statutory orders for art (along with music and physical education) in the final round and the stipulation that art was compulsory only for ages 5 to 14 years, created differentiation across the whole curriculum and between non-core foundation subjects in particular; this created imbalance within a defined curriculum.

Viewed positively, the National Curriculum established that art was to be planned for, and taught to, all children throughout Key Stages 1, 2 and 3, and that it is a subject in its own right. This latter point is significant as in theory it ought not to be possible to reduce art to a subservient, illustrative feature of other areas of the curriculum. Also, to continue in this positive vein, the Non-statutory Guidance (NSG) (1992) is full of good practice and is informing if insubstantial.

This chapter considers the issues raised by the teaching of, and learning in, art for pupils with special needs and some of the possible approaches. It would be useful first to review the aims of art education. The following is from Piotrowski (1995) and is essentially similar to many such attempts. Within the context of primary education, the aims of art education are for the children:

- to develop the skills of art, namely drawing, painting, using colour, printing, modelling, using textiles and textures;

- to develop their visual literacy and appreciation;
- to develop an appreciation of the work of other artists from a variety of cultures and styles;
- to be able to communicate personal responses to art;
- to know and use effectively the language of art: line, colour, tone, shape, pattern, form and texture; and
- to have the opportunity for personal expression and creative endeavour (p. 138).

Art has traditionally been seen as a subject with particular relevance to pupils with special needs. While this is true – it is a subject affording opportunities for all pupils – it is perhaps worth exploring why. There is the curious belief that art is a non-academic subject and therefore must be suitable for so-called non-academic pupils. There is also the belief that the therapeutic aspect of experience in art will be beneficial for children with special needs; an approach to art therapy in a primary school is usefully outlined by Prokofiev (1994). Certainly it is impossible not to be aware of this aspect of art work when, for example, working with clay; clay therapy allows for the engagement of ideas, emotions and images with the material involved in a particularly immediate and dynamic way. The danger of justifying art experience for such children on the basis of its therapeutic properties alone, however, can lead to a disinclination to plan and teach it; a desire not to interfere with the perceived therapy.

Art experience is of enormous benefit to all children, for a large proportion of children with special needs in the mainstream primary classroom it is significantly an area of the curriculum which encourages expression without necessarily the demands of reading and writing. The materials used are of a rich variety and the ways of using the materials are varied offering diverse routes and access to the art curriculum. Children can explore images, emotions and situations in ways afforded uniquely by the arts. My commitment here is to the exploration of the range of opportunities afforded to children with special needs – indeed all children – through experience in art. It is not necessary to take a neurological model and justify art as developing motor skills and co-ordination, nor to adopt the therapeutic model referred to above. Although as Barnett and Henderson (1992) demonstrate in their research into figure drawing by dyspraxic children there are fascinating insights to be gained from studying motor skills. Art experience benefits us all because of the wholeness of the experience; the holistic engagement with an infinite diversity of ideas, materials, processes and techniques.

There are surprisingly few publications in the field of art education and special needs – Mortimer (1994) concurs – a selection of recent ones are listed at the end of this chapter, notably Chantry (1988).

As stated earlier, one major positive implication of National Curriculum art is that it has to be planned and taught for ages 5 to 14 years. There is still the need, however, for careful monitoring of the balance across curriculum subjects for individual pupils. A significant proportion of children, in primary schools, defined as having special needs have difficulties in the acquisition and development of literacy skills. The dilemma facing schools is how to achieve the optimal balance between developing basic skills on the one hand and ensuring breadth of curriculum on the other. All too often in the past, children with special needs were given a restricted curriculum which emphasized the basic skills. The children had a greater concentration of their time spent upon the very areas of learning they found most difficult, with the inherent possibility of reinforcing failure and lowering self-esteem. Most of the literature available – Taylor (1992), Hull (1993) and Mortimer (1994) – emphasizes the fact that experience in art develops both the cognitive and affective learning in the child. Given Taylor's warning (1992) that the arts have been 'squeezed into inadequate timetable slots as other subjects with enhanced National Curriculum clout came on stream' (p. 53), there is a need for the monitoring of individual experience to take place. It is interesting to compare the experience of gifted children in this respect. One of the main approaches for meeting the special needs of exceptionally and very able pupils is the 'widening of the curriculum by means of additional activities or subjects. . .' (Callow, 1994, p. 151). This point underscores the inequality of approaches to curriculum planning for the range of children with special needs. Linked implicitly with this is the spectre of low expectation for the majority of children with special needs. Mortimer (1994) highlights as 'disturbing' Dearing's reference (1993) to the need to have 'realistic expectations' of children with special needs.

Several authors emphasize the significant effect of our level of expectation upon children's learning specifically in this field: Taylor (1992), 'low expectations can still militate against the development of self-esteem. As one Wigan teacher working in special educational provision summarises the problem, 'many see the handicap before the child' (p. 53); Hull (1993) refers to low expectation as being a 'barrier to progress' leading to low achievement; and finally on this point, Mortimer (1994) says: 'One of the key "realistic expectations" that emerged . . . was that we should have no preconceived boundaries to our expectations . . . one of the things that actually disables children is the limitation of our expectations' (p. 222).

APPROACHES

Essentially, the approaches to be explored in this section draw together aspects of good practice. They are the fundamental ways of working which promote access to the curriculum and promote quality interaction. We shall consider issues related to:

- planning
- establishing a developmental approach to artwork
- developing the language of art

Planning

National Curriculum art (NCC, 1992) promotes study in art as a developmental process. Not only is this good practice and an intelligent way to work, but it is of huge benefit to children with special needs. Children with special needs are obviously not a homogenous group but by constantly reviewing and seeking ways of improving our practice generally, we can hope to meet the diversity of special needs presenting in the primary mainstream classroom. The NSG for art (NCC, 1992) has a section on planning and, indeed, there is emphasis throughout the document on careful planning, taking a long-term view to planning and developing the art work through the various stages detailed in the strands. The original strands appear in revised form as Section 7 in the Programmes of Study (POS):

> Pupils should be given opportunities to:
>
> a. record responses, including observations of the natural and made environment;
> b. gather resources and materials, using them to stimulate and develop ideas;
> c. explore and use two- and three-dimensional media, working on a variety of scales;
> d. review and modify their work as it progresses;
> e. develop understanding of the work of artists, craftspeople and designers, applying knowledge to their work;
> f. respond to and evaluate art, craft and design, including their own and others' work.

In NSG (NCC, 1992) there is explicit reference to differentiation and progression as 'two vital elements to consider in planning' (para. 1.8, D4). Planning should:

> clearly build upon previous work and take account of previous achievement. This presupposes,
>
> - planning which is sequential and long term;

- knowing what pupils have done before and how successfully that work has been completed.

The NSG (NCC, 1992) identify three principles which are to guide our planning for progression in art:

  i. the progress of individual pupils needs planning;
  ii. progression is manifested through greater depth of knowledge, broader understanding and applying skills more expertly in increasingly challenging contexts; and
  iii. pupils should develop an ability to select for themselves the methods and materials most appropriate to the task (para. 1.9, D4).

It can be seen from the above that what is intended is not a programme of discrete, prescribed activities each yielding a defined end product.

So what is a developmental approach to art work and how can this assist children with special needs in the mainstream class?

A developmental approach

The initial stimulus may well be related to the firsthand experience of the children: perhaps an aspect of the external environment or an artefact possibly contextualized by a history or geography study unit e.g. a Victorian artefact or an African mask, either would have meaning and relevance to the children. The process followed may well be that the children:

- explore, observe and make sketches, take photographs
- discuss their observations and put their sketches, photographs and 'samples' together into a group or class collection
- develop their ideas into perhaps an individual or group drawing or painting
- in a group, explore other aspects of their collection or translate their original ideas into another medium, e.g. three-dimensional work or using textiles. They may also at this stage – if not at stages 1 or 2 – look at and discuss the work of other artists (children or adults)
- the work from the different groupings may be arranged together as a display of different responses thus celebrating the achievements of individuals and groups to develop further and enrich the children's learning.

Such an approach benefits all the children in the class. It enables children to participate at all stages of the development either as an individual or as a member of a group. The approach encourages and values a divergence of response, there are different roles to be adopted and a variety of grouping strategies are possible. The NSG (1992) planning sheets A and B both support a developmental approach, perhaps model B stresses more visually the development over time. A structured, non-prescriptive approach enabling all children to experience and contribute in a variety of grouping and re-grouping strategies, valuing achievement, encouraging expression and developing personal responsibility is particularly supportive to children with special needs. There are many examples of working in this way in evidence in the Oliver and Boyd Primary Art pack texts (Clement and Page, 1992), the CENSAPE videos (1994) and regular features in Scholastic's *Art and Design* monthly staff-room magazine.

Developing the language of art

In the aims of art education outlined earlier in the chapter, a significant aspect of the planned experience in art is to encourage children's personal expression and to develop their confidence in expressing their response to their own art and that of other people. Children need to develop the language of art to, in turn, develop visual literacy. There is much debate regarding the definition of the term 'visual literacy' and whether it can be taught and assessed, e.g. Allen (1994). In developing the children's visual literacy the teacher is enabling the children to identify, classify and express their responses to art work and to their environment. This requires experiences which develop the language of art (line, colour, shape, tone, pattern, form, texture), give opportunities for the confident use of that language and to compare and contrast different forms, and allow the children to express their responses. Clearly for most children this can be through expressive language, be that spoken, signed or written. For children with significant visual impairment there can be a great diversity of experience achieved through a programme which emphasizes work in three-dimensional forms, texture, textiles and linear designs in relief and applique. There are occasional exhibitions at galleries (e.g. The Whitworth Art Gallery, Manchester), which are designed for the exploration of texture and form specifically to meet the needs of partially sighted and blind visitors.

Teachers' resource centres, galleries and museums have small collections of artefacts which can be borrowed for use in school. This provides essential hands on experience with a range of items representing the range of art forms for developing the appropriate language.

In developing children's confidence in the use of the language of art, there are obvious benefits for the children's language skills across the curriculum; for most these will be oral skills, for some, non-verbal communication.

CASE STUDIES

To conclude this chapter there are two case studies of art work experienced by primary-aged children. The first group of children were aged 7 to 11 years in a moderate learning difficulties unit, the second group of children were from a mainstream class representing the full range of capability.

Case study 1

Joanne was a student teacher on a nine-week teaching practice in a unit for children with moderate learning difficulties. Her topic was to be Ourselves and she decided that the art work would be based on drawing faces. We planned the art work so that the children would do an initial drawing of a friend's face, have a range of related practical experiences and have a repeat attempt at drawing their friend's face four weeks later.

The pre- and post-exposure drawings were completed using the same basic drawing pencil and paper. The practical activities involved included:

- Joanne's own felt board with assorted faces, facial features and hair cut out of felt which the children could layer
- model heads for face painting and 'hairstyling'
- mirrors
- magnifying glasses
- paper and carefully selected portrait colour crayons which were freely available.

The children enjoyed a full range of additional experiences related to the general topic of Ourselves such as the predictable handprinting and the less predictable but hugely enjoyable feetprinting – this takes immense organization with excitable children!

The comparison of the pre- and post-exposure drawings of friend's faces revealed a vast improvement in shape, proportion, number of features and detail of those features. The growth of confidence was also evident through the children's use of scale and position on the page.

Case study 2

Elizabeth's teaching practice was with a Year 4 class in a mainstream school. She was planning her art work on portraits which would complement plans for a history topic on the Tudors and Stuarts. Quite literally, the last thing she asked the children to do was to draw a face. Elizabeth adopted the developmental process whereby the children:

- identified areas of light and dark on faces
- drew in detail one facial feature using a hard lead pencil
- used conte drawing pencils in the range of colours from white through sepia to mahogany to redraw that feature
- used newspaper in a three-dimensional papier mâché effect to build up the feature on a textured piece of card (the insides of brown cardboard boxes!)
- finally drew a face, again, on textured card, as before, using the conte crayons, ordinary chalk and charcoal.

The results were stunning for all children. I have had the work from these children on display, the studies were greeted with enthusiasm and incredulity that the work was from Year 4 pupils and from the full range of children.

The two case studies illustrate the major emphasis of this chapter, that where art work is carefully planned to give structure to the teaching and learning intended, but not a prescription for a defined product, the quality of art work and the learning achieved is greatly enhanced for all children.

REFERENCES

Allen, D. (1994) Teaching visual literacy – some reflections on the term, *JADE*, **13** (2), 133–44.

Barnett, A. and Henderson, S. (1992) Some observations on the figure drawings of clumsy children, *British Journal of Educational Psychology*, **62**, 341–55.

Callow, R. (1994) Classroom provision for the able and the exceptionally able, *Support for Learning*, **9** (4), 151–4.

CENSAPE (1994) Set of three videos with notes from The Centre for the Study of the Arts in Primary Education, University of Plymouth.

Chantry, K. (1988) 'Art and Craft'. In Roberts, T. *Encouraging Expression*. London: Cassell.

Clement, R. and Page, S. (1992) *Primary Art*. Harlow: Oliver & Boyd.

Dearing, R. (1993) *Interim Report: The National Curriculum and its Assessment*. London: HMSO.

Department for Education (DFE) (1994) *National Curriculum: Art for Ages 5–14* (revised orders). London: HMSO.

Department of Education and Science (DES) (1991) *Art in the National Curriculum*. London: HMSO.

Hull, J. (1993) What price the arts in the curriculum?, *Support for learning*, **8** (4), 163–8.

Mortimer, A. (1994) Opportunity not sympathy, *JADE*, **13** (3), 221–33.

National Curriculum Council (NCC) (1992) *National Curriculum Non-statutory Guidance: ART*. London: NCC.

Piotrowski, J. (1995) 'Co-ordinating Art at Key Stage Two'. In Harrison, M.

(ed.) *Developing a Leadership Role within the Key Stage 2 Curriculum.* London: Falmer Press.

Prokofiev, F. (1994) The role of an art therapist, *Art and Craft* (August), 22–3.

Taylor, R. (1992) Art through knowing and understanding, Br. J. Spec. Ed., **19** (2), 53–5.

FURTHER READING

For a comprehensive, regularly updated list contact NSEAD (address on p. 100).

Barnes, R. (1987) *Teaching Art to Young Children 4–9.* London: Routledge.

Gentle, K. (1993) *Teaching Painting in the Primary School.* London: Cassell.

Kellogg, R. (1970) *Analysing Children's Art.* San Francisco: National Press.

Lancaster, J. (1990) *Art in the Primary School.* London: Routledge.

Lancaster, J. (1990) *Art, Craft and Design in the Primary School.* Corsham, Wilts: NSEAD.

Mathieson, K. (1993) *Children's Art and the Computer.* Sevenoaks, Kent: Hodder & Stoughton.

Morgan, M. (1988) *Art 4–11.* London: Simon & Schuster.

National Curriculum Council (NCC) (1990) *The Arts 5–16: Practice and Innovation and a Curriculum Framework.* Harlow: Oliver & Boyd.

Payne, M. (1993) Froebelian principles and the art NC, *JADE*, **12** (2), 179–93.

Piotrowski, J. and Ray, R. (1993) 'Foundation Subject: Art'. In Pumfrey, P. D. and Verma, G., *Cultural Diversity and the Curriculum*, Vol. 3. London: Falmer Press.

Piotrowski, J. (1995) 'Co-ordinating Art at Key Stage Two'. In Harrison, M. (ed.) *Curriculum Co-ordination at Key Stage Two.* London: Falmer Press.

Ray, R. (1995) 'Co-ordinating Art at Key Stage One'. In Davies, J. (ed.) *Developing a Leadership Role within the Key Stage One Curriculum.* London: Falmer Press.

2

Creative writing workshops for all

Rita Ray

Teachers want to help children to become literate. In the case of those children who have problems it might be considered that creative writing should have a low priority until they have learned the basics. Yet primary teachers continue to believe in and see the importance of story and poem making for *all* children.

In this chapter I shall explore the value of creative writing workshops for all children, through a discussion of the workshop approach. How does a workshop differ from a lesson? It is usually a longer session, perhaps half a day, to give children the chance to immerse themselves in themes and activities. Also, there is an apprenticeship feel about a workshop. You are all in it together. The teacher, writer or other 'expert' leads the session in a spirit of discovery along with the children. Materials are prepared so that children have a choice of expressive media. The 'expert' has a bank of stimuli and ideas to draw upon and takes a flexible approach, depending on the group's response.

Here are the comments of a writer, Adele Geras, and the English co-ordinator of a primary school following creative writing workshops. The school had decided to have a literature topic and the writer's visit was part of this context. The teachers had already completed much preparatory work before Adele Geras's visit.

Adele Geras:

> The two days I spent at . . . school were eye openers. Until I went there I really thought that all I did was write stories which, with any luck, would bring some pleasure to their readers. I never realized what inspired teachers could do with these stories, using them in the most imaginative and ingenious ways to teach all sorts of things that hadn't occurred to me as I sat alone with a piece of paper in front of me.
>
> On the first day, I spoke to the children about my work and answered as many questions as I could at the time. I also did two creative writing workshops and was very impressed with the enthusiasm and liveliness of everyone who took part.

English co-ordinator:

Adele's visits to the school gave the children an awareness of the importance of audience and purpose. Not only was their topic on literature shared in school and at home but also with the author herself.

On reflection the staff realized that many other areas of the curriculum had been covered through the literature topic and this gave us confidence to try out other ideas. As a staff we were enriched by the added input and the children developed self-esteem and a respect for one another's writing.

Children with special needs can benefit equally from this kind of input provided the approach is flexible and allows them to take part fully. The projects I have taken part in were based in special schools and special units within mainstream schools; others linked special and mainstream schools. Children with special needs often have to be categorized for purposes of getting support or making suitable teaching programmes. There are, however, few differences to be observed during workshops, especially when several ways of expression and communication are offered. Creative work provides an opportunity for self-expression which frees children who have poor literacy skills and feeds back into the process of acquiring those skills.

As pointed out in a seminal work on the story, *The Cool Web*, 'Narrative is a primary act of mind'. Poems and stories were handed on through the oral tradition long before people were literate. Reading and writing are a means of communicating, not the root of creation nor the source of story and poetry.

WRITERS IN SCHOOL

Teachers often find that a visit from a writer can be a springboard for ideas. There are several kinds of writer-in-school placement. The type and length of placement depends on the sponsor. Schools may have a day's visit, or arts projects run by libraries and LEAs, now very limited, would consist of a longer 'residency', perhaps a half day per week for six weeks in one school or three full days with different schools. Regional arts centres have a list of writers who will visit schools. The Poetry Society, in conjunction with W.H. Smith, organizes a one and a half day workshop followed by a performance and the production of an anthology of the children's work. Preparing and performing work for an audience, even in a small way, can be a confidence booster. In one school, where the teacher knew that the children were unlikely to get the support of a large audience, she organized the performance in a large classroom rather than in a hall. The head and most of the staff turned up to augment the audience, making it enjoyable and memorable for the children.

I use a range of stimulus materials such as masks, puppets and recordings of traditional chants and music from different cultures. Some of the wooden masks go with stories from the oral traditions of North and South America and Asia. There are shadow and carved puppets from the *Ramayana*. These never fail to captivate children. They are always eager to handle them and work with them. Other puppets are of soft materials and represent stock characters for story building. The recordings inspire the children to make up their own chants and raps.

WHAT USE IS CREATIVE WRITING?

Creative writing has been viewed as a psychological outlet. Although, as we shall see later, creative work can be therapeutic there are many more possibilities inherent in making poetry and stories. Here are some intellectual, emotional and therapeutic associations:

1. Poetry can help language development. It can work on rhyme and rhythm and can introduce word play, so increasing knowledge and understanding of vocabulary and grammar.
2. Poetry, stories and role-play can distance situations and allow children to learn to handle practical, everyday situations by acting them out.
3. Using children's spoken language and individual poems and stories in class can increase confidence and show children that their own language is valued and valid in the realm of school.
4. For children who have emotional problems or have undergone trauma of some kind, participation in poems, stories and role play can help them to work out problems in a safe situation as well as simply gaining the pleasure and enjoyment that is vital in rebuilding lives.

As well as taking the above points into consideration, the workshop activities I shall discuss also fulfil the requirements of the Programme of Study for English.

There is still much romanticism attached to poetry and creative writing. This seems to arise from what was believed by some theorists in the sixties – it is axiomatic that all children are creative and you should stand back and let the creativity unfold. This is well illustrated in the opening lines of Gareth Owen's poem, *Miss Creedle teaches creative writing*:

'This morning,' cries Miss Creedle,
'We're all going to use our imaginations . . .

Are we ready to imagine, Darren?
I'm going to count to three.
At one, we wipe our brains completely clean;
At two, we close our eyes;
And at three, we imagine.'

Not surprisingly Miss Creedle's pupils, especially Darren, are not inspired by Miss Creedle's attempts. I can think of many children, and adults, who would respond in the same way when asked to 'close your eyes and imagine' by a Miss Creedle on a grey Monday morning.

Rather than whirling around like Miss Creedle it helps to have a concrete starting point. Real experience or drama provide the best starting points.

In this chapter I shall describe children's work arising from:

- an interactive art exhibition
- a visit to a small zoo
- a series of creative workshops in a residential school for children who have emotional problems which have been linked to their circumstances.

The foregoing work was undertaken as part of a series of creative writing projects which involved linking primary and special schools and working with children who had a variety of special needs, in mainstream and special schools and units. Although these projects were specially organized and funded the teachers reported that they had been enriched by the opportunity of working in a concentrated way and had gained many practical ideas that they could use and develop in future lesson planning.

I shall describe some of the workshops, how the children responded to the various stimuli presented and how they expressed their responses through different modalities and media. The examples are not underpinned by theory – the examples *are* the theory. When I undertook these projects I was not sure of the kind of response to expect from the children I was to work with. I hoped that intuition would be informed by theoretical background and practical experience, but what you need most when you stand before a group of expectant faces is belief – belief in the children and in the 'unrehearsed intellectual adventure' that lies before you all.

POETRY IS ORDINARY LANGUAGE

The Clwyd project

The Clwyd project focused on an art exhibition in the gallery attached to Rhyl library. Groups of children were to visit the exhibition and I would work with them, first in the gallery itself, where there were tables with drawing and writing materials, and then in the children's schools, spending a day in each one. Some of the children were from a special (MLD) school and others from a special class within a primary school. The children's ages ranged from 8 to 11 years.

The exhibition was called *BP re-Vision – New Challenges in Contemporary Art*. The catalogue (1992) describes it as 'a mixed media exhibition which offers the opportunity to appreciate contemporary art on a number of levels'. It consisted of three-dimensional work with many different textures. The works hanging on the walls had raised or textured surfaces and everything could be touched. The exhibition was originally conceived with visually impaired people in mind but as the catalogue points out:

> In recent years there has been a rise in popularity and demand for multi-sensory shows . . . By their very nature they are stimulating and fun, engaging all the senses and rendering art more accessible . . . to everyone.
>
> (Greenwich, LEA, 1992)

This kind of approach was ideal. Being able to touch, interact with and explore the works made the experience complete. Two pieces of work proved to be especially popular with the children – *The Giant's House* and *Light Cave*.

The Giant's House had a giant family's table and chairs made from wood and covered in a straw-like material. A giant's night clothes hung from a chair, there was a drawer full of pottery biscuits and a little cupboard with a pipe and spectacles covered in hessian-type material. There were no actual figures in the sculpture and the children used the clues in the scene to guess how the giants lived and what they did.

Light Cave was, by contrast, an abstract piece of sculpture. The basic shape was a large dodecahedron made of mirrors. One face had been removed so that the children could put their heads inside and see reflections everywhere. There were fibre optic lights, constantly changing colour, inside. The outside was covered with a thick shaggy sheepskin which had stones and shells tied to it. The sculptor, Jan O'Highway, writes:

> Ideas come in response to a place or situation, to express strong feelings, sometimes just from playfulness. Touch is very important, and sound. One of the reasons I love using shells is the clicking noise they make when they touch each other.
>
> The sculpture for re-Vision combines organic materials and light in the form of fibre optics. The pulsing lights give the illusion of

movement and life within the dense, tactile outer covering. It's meant to be a piece to be enjoyed . . .

I was interested in capturing the children's language in response to the exhibits, on the spot. Many children who struggle with language find it hard to discuss and describe in the classroom. Confronted by stimuli in a real situation it's natural to share, enjoy and comment. The children's spontaneous speech in context is often a better reflection of what they can express than their attempts to contribute in classroom discussion.

They love listening to themselves on tape and can reflect on a situation in this way. Although video films are useful, listening to audiotape helps the children to focus on language and to identify and recall events through the words they hear. There are further interesting things that can be done with the transcript. The children's words can be used as captions in display, to make brochures and stories about visits and to make group poems.

To make a poem from the transcripts I organize the remarks, doing some prior selection. This helps to cut down the amount of transcript we have to go through together and makes it possible to highlight interesting comments.

Here are some of the children's comments about the giant family exhibit:

Where's the giant?
Is that coat the giant's?
It smells nice.
I can smell Christmas.
Pretend the giant's up there chasing us.
Help me! The giant's getting me!
Come in the giant's castle.
Is it made of paper?
Is his jacket very big?
He's a nice giant.
Are these his fags?
Isn't he greedy?
Are these pretending buttons?
He eats his buttons as well.
And he's been chewing his dressing gown.
The giant's money bag.
Jack took it.
The giant's hat comes to life like this . . . doo dee doo dee doo.
The giant wears it.
It gives him his food. It gives him biscuits and it dances for him. What does he eat in the morning?
Paul's found a big spoon.
WOW!
A giant can't eat with that spoon.
It's too prickly.

Straw's been stuck on it – like a witch's spoon.
She stirs up spiders and elephants.
His glasses make you blind.

The children are joining in make believe and making inferences about the giant's personality and lifestyle. Although the language above isn't Shakespeare or Keats it is an achievement for the children concerned. To work with their own words is meaningful as well as a boost to self-esteem. Even in this short extract from the transcript possibilities for development can be seen. In addition to captions and a group poem there is the story of the giant's hat to be extended into a class story with illustrations. The 'hat' was not part of the exhibition but had been improvised by one of the children from a large sheet of sugar paper. The children put some biscuits into the giant's dressing gown pocket 'in case he gets hungry in the night'. These spontaneous bits of drama and role-play, invented on the spot with the giant props and setting, could be developed later into little plays and stories.

Artists retain a strong appreciation of the senses and of 'playfulness'. Children identify with this and the groups threw themselves into the enjoyment of *Light Cave* without questioning what it was meant to be. They buried their faces in the sheepskin, rattled the shells and stones, took turns at putting their heads inside to watch the coloured lights change and to try out the acoustics. Here is part of the transcript:

It might be a panda's fur, or a polar bear.
Might be a wolf.
I could go to sleep on here.
Like a caveman.
Just put your voice in there.
Wooooooooooooooooooooooooooooooooo
Helloooooooooooooooooooooooooooooo
It's a spaceship.
Is it for shouting in?
Let's make it scarier.
Different colours going round.
What are they made out of?
How did they make holes in the stones?
My cousin broke all his teeth.
It echoes if you shout loud.
Lovely lights.
You can use them for Christmas.
It's changing colour.
Gold see.
It's the giant's gold.
It's danger when it's red.
Danger! Danger! A giant!

We made a long group poem from their comments about the light cave. I made a dodecahedron from silver card, with one face missing, like the light cave. We folded the poem concertina-wise and stuck one end inside the silver shape so the poem could be pulled out and read.

In the gallery the children drew whatever had inspired them and at the end of the session showed what they had done and told the group about it, or asked an adult to tell the group about it.

One group followed up the theme of giants and monsters with their teacher and we developed this theme on the day I worked with them. Another group was inspired by an improvised model theatre I showed them. We had started to make card characters in the gallery. They followed up this theme, making their own theatres from boxes so that we could work on their plays on my visit to school. Among this group was a child in a wheelchair who, because of the nature of the exhibition, had been able to participate fully. The exhibits were within her reach, she could lean forward and call into the light cave and manoeuvre her chair around the giant's furniture. The class teachers and helpers supported the whole project with great enthusiasm, encouraging the children at every stage.

The Wigan project

In recent years there have been some outstanding and extensive arts projects and placements taking place in Wigan schools. One of these was a writer-in-school project which covered all special schools and linked special schools with mainstream schools. The outcome of the project was to be an exhibition and performance when the schools would come together to meet and show what they had done. Several writers were involved in the project. It gave me the opportunity to work with children who had a range of special educational needs. Their schools were categorized as catering for a) severe learning difficulties, b) moderate learning difficulties, c) physical handicap, and d) emotional and behavioural difficulties, though the latter was in fact a residential school, usually for short-term placements, for children who had suffered emotional trauma through difficult life circumstances. Many of the children were being gradually introduced back into mainstream schooling.

With the children who had severe learning difficulties or profound physical disability I used puppets to build up stories and make books. The children enjoyed holding the puppets, sometimes with help, and taking part in the improvised story, usually with a repetitive theme that they could recognize and join in. I shall, however, concentrate on the two longest residences. These placements were each of one half day per week for six weeks. (I have changed the names of the schools.)

Cameron School (MLD). In this Year 5 group all but one of the children could dictate a simple story and some could attempt their own writing. The child who couldn't manage a story usually gave one word responses. She liked trying to copy what she had dictated so had some concept of writing. There were two sources of stimulus for the activities – an outing to a small local zoo and, linked to the animal theme, some carved animal masks which came from Bali.

The class teacher was very involved throughout. He set down his expectations of the residency in a report:

> I wanted the children's work to be related to the Programme of Study for Writing. In our first meeting we picked out some learning objectives that we felt could possibly be achieved by the children. However, I am a firm believer in presenting the children with experiences that are enjoyable. For me, the residency will have been a success if the children, through their experience, have an enjoyable time writing.

For the zoo visit we used the same technique as in the Clwyd project, taking a tape recorder and using the children's own comments to make a group poem. The child who usually gave one word responses in class produced whole sentences in this more stimulating and spontaneous situation. This group really enjoyed listening to themselves and deciding what was to go into the group poem. They included some of the notices that they had read aloud – not always accurately! One of the sentences they chose wasn't grammatical – 'We saw them animals with antlers'. Teachers debate about whether, and when, you should correct grammar and we surely don't want to patronize children and compound their learning problems by keeping them in the dark and not correcting them. I prefer to decide each case individually in context, and to have stepped in and corrected this while these children were bubbling over with the excitement of making their poem would have put a damper on things. The grammar could be tackled at another time in another context. Here is an extract from the group poem:

> DO NOT TOUCH OR FEED THESE ANIMALS
> They bite
> They're vicious
>
> They have these massive white birds
> They're really white
> They're whiter than snow
>
> The tiny monkey's riding on its back
>
> PLEASE DO NOT KNOCK ON THE GLASS
> Oh, isn't he beautiful?
> He stinks as well
> He looks like a dog

He looks like a big, bad wolf
Does he stay there all night?

LOOK BUT DO NOT PUT YOUR FINGERS IN
We have to go back to the bus
Did you see the giraffes?
Did you see the horse?
Did you see the donkey?

We saw them animals with antlers
We saw peacocks and baboons
We've seen the kangaroos and owls
We even saw the fish
But Miss, you missed the camels

In the 'mask' session the children were keen to handle the masks and after we had shared some ideas they worked in pairs or individually with a chosen mask. Some attempted to write down their thoughts. Occasionally children who find writing difficult lose confidence and need a lot of reassurance. One boy, John, made a good start on a poem about a wild boar's mask but suddenly hid under the table and, in no uncertain terms, said he wasn't doing any more. Sometimes a glimpse of success can be as unnerving as a taste of failure. One of my best moments was seeing this big, shy boy stand up in front of all the children from other schools and say his poem, to enthusiastic applause, at the end of the project.

The children illustrated the poems and made a class anthology. As part of the project, we made several small printed copies of the anthology and 'launched' it officially at the final exhibition and presentation. Here are some examples:

The Frog

The frog's eyes stick out. He lives
in the freezing water. He opens and
shuts his mouth. He is jumping up
and down. The frog eats flies and
fishes. He goes to sleep in the
dark.

by Dawn

The Demon Pig

A pig is fat and a pig is hungry
He eats chicken bits
He's got ugly eyes
He can kill people with his fangs
He's a bad pig
He's a wild pig

He's a demon pig

by John

Lesa's Dog

Lesa's dog wags his tail
Lesa's dog has four legs
Lesa's dog has yellow coloured hair
Lesa's dog is a big dog
Lesa's dog has big teeth
Lesa's dog has lots of hair
Leas's dog likes doggy food
Leas's dog sometimes has chips
Lesa's dog is called Prince

by Lesa

Dinky the Dinosaur

Dinky was walking down the path and
eating an apple. He went brown and
green and his eyes went together
and he cried and went home to daddy
dinosaur. His spikes went red and
daddy dinosaur said, 'You are
dying' and put him in bed. In the
morning he died. Daddy and mummy
were crying and they took him to
the grave and buried him. Then they
went home.

by Brian

Like Dawn, Brian had ideas about what a poem looked like and how many words should go on a line. His poem about Dinky, based on a fierce-looking dragon mask, became very popular and was made into a class play.

Greenhill School (residential). The children at Greenhill live in small units, about eight children per unit. Each unit has bedrooms, bathrooms, a living room, a kitchen and a classroom. The care staff and teachers all take part in class work and the children call the staff by their first names. The group I was to work with consisted of seven boys aged 10 to 15 years, working in a primary setting, i.e., in their own classroom, mainly with one teacher and adopting a thematic approach to Key Stage 2 and Key Stage 3 Programmes of Study, with most of the group attaining level 2–3 in core subjects.

In keeping with the philosophy of the school the boys were asked if they wanted to take part in the project. One of them looked at me blankly and said, 'We're dead hard, us. You don't want to work with us', giving a hint of the very low self-esteem experienced by this group. However, they decided to give it a try. They sat far apart in separate, single desks. Normally, at the beginning of a first workshop, some time would be spent getting to know one another and then I would read some poetry, but giving a poetry reading didn't seem to be the thing to do here and a positive start was vital. The head of the school had told me that the boys enjoyed design technology and making things so I decided to make this a starting point. One way of doing this was to design a character. We cut up animal names and put the syllables together to make a new creature, for example, baboon, tiger and crocodile became 'crocotiboon'. The main advantages of creating such characters are a) they are completely new and unknown, so the child can create a world that does not rely on prior knowledge, and b) the character and stories can be developed to any level. Some children create simple stories, others have created complex worlds with their own languages and with details such as height, weight and speed of the creature.

They drew their characters on card and cut them out. They drew backgrounds for their characters on larger pieces of card, cut a slit in the picture and moved their characters back and forth along the slit, making up scenes and dialogue for them. We got as far as recording some of the dialogue and fortunately the mix of practical and creative was such that each could take part at his own level, making the animated pictures more technical or the stories more complex. I could tell that after the first flush of success the boys might lose confidence and tear up their pieces of work so I said I wanted to save them for the exhibition and took their work away with me.

Despite being shy and hesitant at first it was obvious that they enjoyed using the tape recorder. We went out to a large local park with a pets' corner and took photographs and made recordings. One of the funniest recordings was a commentary they improvised on a playful fight between two piglets. They improvised the commentary in the style of the wrestling matches they saw on television. This group was particularly keen on power figures.

On subsequent visits the boys focused on two main ways of presenting stories – 'shape' books and tape slide shows. Some of them used both means of presenting the same story. They especially liked the 'door' book shape, i.e. a book cut in such a way that each page opens like a door, leading you through the story. We made two kinds of slides by drawing directly on to the clear slide with non-toxic overhead projector pens or putting drops of food colouring, glycerine and tiny bits of thread on to the slide to get a 'mystery picture'. We projected the mystery pictures on to a screen and decided what they could be and made up stories about them. The boys usually saw fairly gory monsters and we had one long story about a snakespider. The door books gave a physical structure to their stories, providing that supportive framework that can spur on a child who lacks confidence.

Examples by Max and Craig from Greenhill are shown below.

After making several 'door' books, Max gained enough confidence to invent modifications, such as interactive signs and little 'pop-ups':

**************THE MYSTERY AT 666**************

I saw another trap door. I went through it.
I hit my head on a metal door.
It said, 'What is in the hall?'

(Answer here ————>)

I answered. They opened.
I walked for a minute. I stopped at a lake of lather.
I said, 'How will I get across?'
I saw a sign saying, 'PULL'. So I did.
Stairs appeared. I went up them.
I saw piles of gold.
BANG!!! The door had closed.
I ran to the next door.
I ran through a very small door.
I went through the back door.

THE END

by Max

Craig's story was a tape/slide show. It typifies the strong moral strand running through most of the work in this group:

WILD LIFE

One sunny morning in April I went diving
in the deep blue sea.

There was another chap there too.
He was trying to kill the whales and I
swam up quickly.

He had his harpoon in his hand. He was
trying to trap them in a net.

They tried to get away. Some got away but
others were trapped.

The whales were crying as they were dying. It was sad.

I sneaked up behind him but too late. His mate said, 'Look out!'

I felt pain in my leg. Blood was pouring
out of the wound.

I couldn't do any more. I turned away upset.

I went home and went to the doctor and reported it to the
police and gave them clues.

They caught them and put them in jail.

by Craig

As I remarked earlier 'the examples are not underpinned by
theory, the examples are the theory', so I shall not attempt to draw
lofty conclusions, but would simply reflect that at one level poetry-
and story-making can provide a day's pleasure and fulfilment, while
at another level it can help to return a child to life.

REFERENCES

Greenwich LEA (1992) *BP re-Vision: New Challenges (1992) in Contemporary
Art.* London: London Borough of Greenwich.
Department of Education and Science (DES) (1990) *English 5–16.* London:
HMSO.

FURTHER READING

Bell, C. (1993) *Helping Young Children to Become Writers.* Crediton, Devon:
Southgate.
Corbett, P. and Moses, B. (1986) *Catapults and Kingfishers.* Oxford: Oxford
University Press.
Count to Five and Say I'm Alive, Team Video Productions, Camelot, 222 Kensal
Road, London W10 5BN. Funded by Westminster City Council and
produced in association with Paddington Arts.
Merrick, B. and Balaam, J. (1989) *Exploring Poetry 5–8.* Sheffield: NATE
Publications.
Merrick, B. (1991) *Exploring Poetry 8–13.* Sheffield: NATE Publications.

3

Drama

Andy Jones, Gill Payne and John Rainer

The following chapter addresses the place, nature and forms of drama in education in relation to the primary school curriculum and within the context of the education of children with special educational needs. First, the current place of drama within the English National Curriculum is outlined, and recent supportive references pinpointed. Second, the notion of learning simultaneously in and through drama is analysed, with important and current theoretical issues being explored. Finally, examples of practical drama forms and conventions are succinctly described, as are illustrations of specific activities.

As an educational phenomenon, the art form of drama provides a diverse range of opportunities for teaching and learning. This diversity can enable drama to function as a flexible, varied learning methodology in which all children may achieve, irrespective of age or ability. Drama operates at kinaesthetic, emotional and sensory, as well as intellectual, levels, with potential for any of these to be given specific focus or encouragement within a particular drama. The teacher utilizing drama effectively should be able to provide opportunities for all, to engage in a creative artistic activity, and to learn. As Sue Jennings, writing from a dramatherapy perspective, highlights: 'Drama can help all of us, if we choose to explore its potential' (1986, p. v). More recently, Melanie Peter has also proposed 'a framework for one approach in drama for all pupils' (1994, p. viii).

In what follows we seek to provide a starting point for all primary school teachers interested in exploring such notions.

DRAMA AND THE NATIONAL CURRICULUM

> Drama enables children to reconsider their feelings and attitudes in the light of shared experience. Drama provides a valuable way of learning about oneself and others.
>
> (DES, 1990, pp. 3–6)

Throughout the initial National Curriculum subject documents, references were included to indicate drama methods that teachers could utilize to attain targets and teach subjects (NCC, 1990). It became necessary for non-specialist primary teachers already grappling with the complexities of diversity, differentiation and testing, to understand and use dramatic methodology. The terms 'role-play', 'imaginative play', 'in-role', 'collaborative' and 'exploratory' play, 'improvised drama', 'simulation' and 'group drama' were scattered throughout the subject documents and teachers were encouraged to use them effectively. The most recent National Curriculum document for English states:

> Pupils should be given opportunities to participate in a wide range of drama activities including improvisation, role-play and the writing and performance of scripted drama.
>
> (DFE, 1995, p. 11)

The art form of drama occurs in schools in a variety of contexts. Her Majesty's Inspectorate (HMI) state:

> Drama in schools is a practical, artistic subject. It ranges from children's structured play, through classroom improvisations and performances of specially devised material to performances of Shakespeare.
>
> (HMI, 1989, p.1)

More recently, John Somers attempts:

> to elevate and make more central the role of drama in relation to other subjects, both in day-to-day liaison between teachers of drama and other subject specialists who may see drama as an ideal way to enhance the teaching of their own specialism . . .
>
> (Somers, 1994, p. 9)

However, he sees drama 'as a catalyst and focus in major curriculum projects which may culminate in performance' (Ibid., p. 10).

The findings of HMI recognize that:

> where . . . those with specialist expertise . . . have worked in schools and with teachers, more advantageous and in-depth work has resulted. This work reveals that primary children are capable of achieving far more from the teaching of drama than is often supposed. It also shows the benefits that imaginative teaching of drama can have on many other aspects of the curriculum.
>
> (HMI, 1990, p.8)

When observing play and role-play the inspectorate state that:

> Often only an initial stimulus was required for very young children to slip into role, but, as children matured, they made more conscious use of observation and identified more closely with the individuals involved in plot or story. They gradually acquired the ability to select the relevant skills which sustain dramatic activity.
>
> (Ibid., p. 10)

DRAMA AND LEARNING

When children participate in drama they are engaged in a process which places them in a direct relationship with two disparate, but familiar, elements – the world of play on the one hand, and the world of theatre on the other. Participation in drama is participation in a shared, enacted fiction, structured and focused through conventions borrowed from theatre and media, and driven by principled teacher intervention. As such, drama is familiar territory to any teacher who has observed young children at play in the playground, or provided opportunities and context for play in the classroom (Jones and Reynolds, 1992).

However, for us, it is this notion of 'principled teacher intervention' which helps distinguish drama from 'dramatic play'. While children's dramatic play may be characterized by its spontaneity, we feel that drama as defined here is more likely to be a product of pre-planning. Intervention in this sense is principled because it is always informed by the educational needs of the class.

In a similar way, it is the skilful teacher's conscious use of theatre form which differentiates drama from 'structured play'. In structured play teachers may readily intervene, but they are less likely to promote a particular kind of self-consciousness: what the group is doing is 'making a play' as opposed to 'playing'. Artistic intention on the part of the teacher is often a characteristic of the most exciting work.

This two–fold emphasis places children's drama clearly within the realms of both art and education: for drama to achieve its true potential, a tension between the two should always be present – although emphasis will, of course, vary according to curricular context.

Drama's position between the two realms is, of course, shared with other arts-based areas of the curriculum. What makes drama unique, and where it derives its potency as a learning medium, is a third element derived from the fact of its enaction.

A child participating in drama is inhabiting two 'worlds' simultaneously – the world of the drama, and the 'real' world. This dualism – referred to by Augusto Boal as 'metaxis' (1979, p. 8) – means, in effect, that within the emotional, physical and intellectual engagement brought about by the experience of drama – and importantly in reflecting on it afterwards – the child is able to perceive elements of real life thrown into relief by the events, metaphors and symbols of the drama and vice versa. And, as the fictional contexts available through drama are infinitely variable, this dialectic can provide access to an infinite variety of opportunities for children to construct meaning from their experiences.

More specifically, through this process, where children are involved in negotiating the meaning of the fictions that they have created communally, engagement in drama can stimulate learning of a very particular kind. Drama cannot be content-free; it has to be 'about something', and the material for classroom drama can be drawn from the widest range of sources. But, whatever the content of the drama, children's engagement with it often takes an exploratory form. Within the aesthetic context provided by 'making a play', it stimulates the raising of questions, the solving of problems, the clarification (and challenge) of values, and the gaining of insight into human motivation and the consequences of action.

This kind of learning, therefore, is affective as well as intellectual, and is more related to the raising of consciousness than the inculcating of propositional knowledge. This emphasis in the work has been referred to as 'drama for understanding' (Bolton, in Jackson (ed.), 1993, p. 44) and one of its outcomes as a 'heightened awareness', and it is obviously of central importance when discussing the inclusion of drama on the curriculum – particularly for those pupils who, in the widest sense, have 'special needs'.

And yet, there is more that drama does, and does well. The process is a complex one, and any attempt to provide a model of the areas of learning it may develop is inevitably problematic. Nevertheless, Figure 3.1 is an attempt to do so.

Drama and Learning

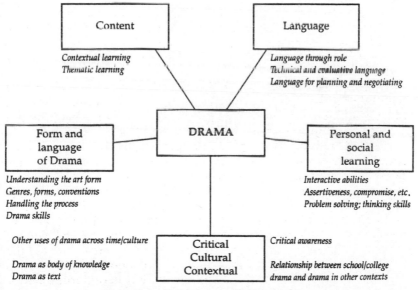

Figure 3.1 *Model of areas of learning for drama*

Content

As has already been described, learning in drama is often centred upon the exploration of content material brought from other areas of the curriculum, and contained and focused through the fictional context of the dramatic engagement itself. Children engage with the fiction as if it were real, and therefore the children's responses – the emotions felt, language evoked and the challenge to their thinking which may result are real, not fictional!

'Content' learning engendered in this engagement may be on a number of levels, often simultaneously present in the work. For instance, in a drama based in a historical context, some of the teacher's aims may well be concerned with fostering a greater understanding of the particular period in which the drama is 'set'. On a literal level, this drama is about, say, the Vikings, and some of the learning may be rooted in a very specific sense of time and place: 'contextual' learning.

It may also explore questions which, because they are concerned with human motivation, might be regarded as having a more 'universal' quality (Heathcote, in Johnson and O'Neill (eds) 1984, p. 103). What it might have 'felt like' to be an 'alien' in a strange and hostile land, or speculation as to how a particularly beautiful Viking brooch might have come to be made by these 'barbarians' (Fines, described in Rainer *et al.*, 1989, p. 11) might be learning outcomes that have some of this universal quality. In this way, the context for the drama often serves as a vehicle into another kind of learning, often related to themes or issues raised within the work: 'thematic' learning.

As dramatic meaning is often sensed through symbol and metaphor, learning of a very particular – and definitely non-literal – potency is possible. Even for quite young children, the fact that the 'young Viking' would rather die than give away the brooch her 'mother' made for her, imbues the brooch with meaning far beyond the object itself, meaning which young people might come to recognize and value in their own lives.

Form and language

Not unreasonably, one would expect young people who regularly 'do' drama to get better at 'doing' it. However, this area is not without its controversies. In recent years a series of debates have ensued, between advocates of 'theatre' on the one hand and 'drama' on the other – or between those who see their job as promoting learning 'in' or 'about' drama, rather than learning 'through' it. We take the view that the s , ...un is artificial and unhelpful, preferring to stress the point that whether the emphasis is on children performing, or on children experiencing, the drama process is fundamentally the same.[1] Whatever the emphasis, it is the process of drama – understanding its elements and knowing how to use them – that we would see as the key to progression in the subject.[2]

Within this area is also subsumed what would be traditionally regarded as 'theatre' and 'technical' skills – the ability of individuals to utilize their understanding of the way in which drama is structured in order to make dramas of high quality. What we would say, however, is that understanding of the form and language of drama is most fruitfully developed through the active making and appraising of drama itself, rather than through decontextualized skills training.

Personal and social learning

Drama is fundamentally a social activity – consequently, it takes its strength from the group dynamic. One aim of many practitioners is the development of better 'social health' in the class (Wagner, 1977, p. 227), and the kind of insight accrued by the participants of successful drama work often develops a particularly strong sense of group identity. By its very nature it involves participants in negotiation and planning; in assertion and compromise; in the clarification of individual and group values and in the sharing of meaning – again, uniquely, on a real and a fictional level.

In the past, because of its emphasis on matters of social value, and the extraordinary power of its communality, drama in schools has sometimes been seen as a panacea for correcting social deprivation or maladjustment. A protracted programme of drama work with a particular group may well have profound effects in promoting positive group feeling and interaction, however, it is probably the case that, in the short term at least, children whose antisocial behaviour has a negative effect on 'normal' classroom activities will have an equally negative effect on drama lessons. One element in this is the particularly demanding nature of drama interactions.

To be truly effective, negotiation in drama does not simply take place between pupils, but also, importantly, between pupils and their teachers, which inevitably involves the 'handing over' of a certain amount of power from teacher to learner. In addition, where teachers themselves participate in the drama – through conventions such as 'teacher in role' (see p. 34) – in order to help structure and focus it, they may empower their classes, at least for the duration of the drama, by the adoption of roles which allow them to interact with their class in ways which are radically different to their usual teaching style. This factor, which places very real demands upon learners and teachers, is paradoxically, a particularly exciting aspect of drama's power as a learning medium: in this way drama has the potential, at least, to transform classroom relationships.

Through its clear antipathy to a 'banking' model of education (Friere, 1972, p. 45) drama creates space for an alternative paradigm for teaching and learning to be developed: one in which teacher and learner are much less bound by the notion that teacher knows the outcome in advance. In this respect drama in education has been described as 'highly processual' and the subject of continual negotiation and renegotiation between participants (O'Toole, 1992, p. 2). This can be profoundly exciting for some teachers; profoundly upsetting for others. For children with learning difficulties, who might already find it difficult to relate to adults, this change in relationship – in the short term – can be unsettling; in the longer term, with a little perseverance, liberating.

Critical, cultural and contextual knowledge

In some respects it is this element of learning in drama which has been overlooked in schools, and which, arguably, needs the most development.

Within this area of learning we would hope that children would be encouraged to see the relationships between the various uses of drama – across time and culture. That, on a basic level what they are involved in – as they improvise their classroom dramas – has a relationship with what they might witness on a visit to a professional theatre, or during a visit from a touring Theatre in Education or Young People's Theatre company; that they understand that drama has existed in all cultures and that it has a variety of manifestations and purposes; that it exists as a body of text on a library shelf, but also, through television, as a cultural form patronized by millions of people, many of whom would not dream of setting foot in a theatre building.

It is our feeling that this kind of awareness in children is crucial if drama is once again to be seen as an important cultural force in society.

Language

As far as the National Curriculum is concerned drama mainly derives its status as an agent in the 'delivery' of elements of English (DFE, 1995, pp. 1–20). In the succession of documents emanating from the DES/DFE, as we have seen, the view of drama presented is largely instrumental. Drama tends to be seen as a means of promoting a language curriculum which is somewhat narrowly defined. Many practitioners would acknowledge, however, that drama – because of its ability to provide learners with contexts for language use outside of their usual, 'real' contexts – can enrich children's language in a wide variety of ways.

Although language development through drama largely derives its efficacy through the concept of role, there are other important aspects to drama's contribution to language development. First, learning of any kind does not seem to happen simply through experience, but also through reflecting on that experience. Some of this reflection may be private, and a skilful teacher will also enable his or her group to use the medium itself for this purpose. Some of this reflection will be public, particularly that related to more 'public', presentational dramas.

An important part of any drama curriculum must be therefore to equip children, from an early stage in their development, with a critical vocabulary which might enable them to describe and appraise not only their own work, but also the work of others – peers and professionals (Nicholson, 1994, p. 21). Without this, it is surely unlikely that children presented with abstract or challenging dramas will be able to engage meaningfully with the work, or effectively communicate their feelings about it to others – and in so doing compare their 'reading' of the drama's meaning, as well as more technical aspects, with others'.

Finally, drama, in common with other areas of the curriculum, has its own technical vocabulary – the use of the word 'role' itself is a case in point – and again we would hope that teachers would seek to enable pupils to refer knowledgeably to the conventions and techniques used during drama lessons or witnessed during performances.

Confidence in language – in describing drama – is surely a first step towards confidence in controlling and manipulating the art form.

THE MEDIUM OF DRAMA

The medium of drama is eclectic and entirely available to all teachers – a creative art form which can appear in many guises within schools' practice. As we have seen, the versatility of drama enables a range of rich educational opportunities – which the teacher new to drama may develop within their practice. What follows is a brief, descriptive overview of the available conventions which exist in educational drama. The teacher should, ideally, become familiar with all such practices in order that the educational scope of drama becomes as fruitful as possible. Beginning with one or two approaches may be the best way to start.

Within individual lessons, mini-projects and/or longer schemes of work, the effective teacher will manipulate the various forms of the medium as and when appropriate employing particular conventions for specific purposes. For the teacher, an ability to feel comfortable with the full range of conventions in drama is clearly beneficial while working within a creative, often self-evolving process. Opportunities offered by the drama conventions allow for spontaneity while pursuing teaching and learning aims, providing the teacher and pupils with a genuinely creative experience. Additionally, children should be offered a mixed, balanced diet of drama activities which avoids staleness and gives full potential to creative, artistic development.

Drama conventions

Tableau/freeze frames/still photographs: relatively easily attainable still images which either individuals or groups create on a given theme or title (e.g. 'The Beach'; 'Friendship'; 'Revenge'). The making of such pictures enables pupils to develop a variety of skills such as concentration, stillness and focus while creating meaning. Pictures can initiate and develop narrative, encapsulate an idea, belief or message in an accessible form which encourages reflection. Children may benefit from opportunities to improve as tableau-makers, as first attempts may be less powerful than later efforts. Allowing a lot of time per image, however, may be unnecessary; some excellent images can be created in a matter of seconds. Discussion and scrutiny of others' images encourages critical awareness and empowers children to see art as a material for their interpretation.

Mimed activity/moving pictures: in film terminology could be seen as 'opening shots' or a 'panoramic view'. Children create silent dramatic action which highlights aspects of the current drama context or class topic (e.g. 'The Ship' or 'Celebration'). This animated overview may be created by individuals, pairs, small groups or the whole class and as with its frozen counterpart, active discussion and scrutiny leads to deeper understanding of both the expressed meaning and the drama form itself. Skills of focus and concentration here become bound with those of precision and clarity of physical expression. As in other conventions, the teacher can stop the drama and encourage the children to improve particular aspects before continuing. The 'perfect' or 'finished' picture need not exist.

Thought-tracking/inner thoughts/hot-seating: individuals may be selected by the teacher, at which point they speak, in role, thoughts about their current situation or activity. This may be achieved while frozen or moving within any drama activities and the teacher may attempt to allow a range of 'roles' to speak in order to gain a comprehensive view of group feelings. 'Hot-seating' allows the group and the teacher to question a particular child in role on the 'hot seat'. They may ask questions regarding the background, feelings, attitudes and thoughts of the character in relation to any stage of the drama. Characters' statements will vary from child to child, ranging from the purely descriptive to the sensitively reflective. As with all drama conventions, children may need time and opportunity to develop oral expression and character identity.

Oral improvisation/simulations/paired or small group role-play: these are perhaps the most regularly used forms of educational drama which allow for children to play roles in both verbal and non-verbal form. Role-play essentially forms the mainstay of much drama work with younger children, and differs from 'acting' as it is mainly concerned with the child 'experiencing' as opposed to 'impersonating' or 'performing' (Neelands, 1984, p. 6).

Interestingly, young children normally have little or no fear of role play as they have relatively few negative experiences of 'performance' compared with some adults. Conversely, through working in role-play children are being encouraged to develop good theatrical awareness via a safe, non-threatening and child-led framework. Children effectively 'play' in role as other people and this enables them to gain insight to and empathy with the feelings, attitudes, joys or horrors of those whose roles they are taking. Role-play is a highly structured 'game', a safe environment within which children may explore the human condition 'through imagined experience' (Neelands, 1992).

Any topic or context may be explored through role-play either within the classroom itself or within any available space (e.g. 'POW Camp' or 'The Medieval Market'). Role-play can be used in various activities within drama sessions, for example, issue-led public meetings, interviews, given scenarios, court scenes, press conferences, deputations over workplace crises, teaching another to do a job or demonstrating skills to an interested audience.

Presentations/performances/assembly/documentaries: individuals, pairs, small groups or whole classes of children may work towards creating drama for presentation which is shared with either members of their class, other pupils in the school or the wider community. It is important to stress that the ideas, images, words and structures created through 'classroom' drama can easily become content for presentation. When skilfully focused, the collective minds of a class are very capable of creating powerful performance work.

Mantle of the expert: a variation of role-play and a particular approach developed by Dorothy Heathcote and Gavin Bolton during the 1970s and 1980s (Bolton, 1979, p. 67). The class becomes engaged in a task which requires, in an imagined context, that they are experts in a given field or area of knowledge. A newspaper office, for example, may become the context for drama focusing upon an air crash where survivors may or may not be found. The teacher in this drama convention prepares a range of activities, all of which demand 'expert' skills from the children in role as writers, designers, photographers, etc. They may be required to interview key people, write leading stories, create necessary pictures and produce a readable paper, all to a tight 'print deadline'. During such activity the teacher may intervene to add further complications or requirements to the task before allowing the drama to recommence. The drama can also incorporate other activities such as public meetings, press conferences or mimed activities.

Teacher in role: also developed as a convention of drama in education by Dorothy Heathcote and Gavin Bolton. In this convention, the teacher participates in role and consequently steers or guides the drama 'from within'. The teacher does not necessarily need to relinquish authority or control of the class through the use of teacher in role: roles may be selected which, in status terms, differ little from that of teacher and allow control to be maintained, e.g. The Judge, Expedition Leader, Managing Director of the Company, The Storyteller, Keeper of the Gate or simply a teacher from a different school. It is important to stress that the drama can always be stopped and the ground rules re-established if the work needs re-focusing. The use of the convention of teacher in role easily blends with the other conventions described above.

We have included two short examples of practical work below.

A Year 6 class with wide knowledge of the Victorian era were interested in the plight of homeless children. Through a drama session they produced a still image of children on the streets and their thoughts were 'tracked'. Coming out of role they designed a workhouse on large sheets of paper and based on their thoughts as street children they created their own personal history, which had resulted in homelessness. The hall now became the workhouse, and the class, the inmates. Dramatic tension was introduced by the teacher in role as a harsh workhouse manager who constantly presented obstacles for them to confront, e.g. a girl who had the skills and expertise as a seamstress was instructed to catch rats in the cellar, a male chimney sweep was allocated to ironing duty. Further dramatic conflict was introduced by a second teacher in role (played by the headteacher) as a beneficent visitor with whom the inmates had no opportunity to voice their complaints.

At the end of the session during debriefing, the children demonstrated a depth of understanding of the circumstances of children of a bygone era in relation to their own lives. Even the less confident children were part of the action and made significant contributions. As one usually reticent child remarked, 'that was a story and we were in it'.

The children had ownership of the story and the intervention of the teacher in role was only necessary to heighten the drama and introduce awe, tension and climax. As John Somers states:

> The only imperative is that the conflict or tension which will energise the drama is clearly identified within the material and captured in the drama.
> (Somers, 1994, p. 13)

The second example is from drama undertaken with Year 2 children on the effects that climatic changes and population growth have upon a group of people living in a valley in a region afflicted by drought, thus illustrating drama can be successfully utilized within cross-curricular thematic work.

The children designed a village and discussed the roles of the people who would live there, unaware at this point that change would occur. Having established the context they began to enact their roles through 'working' in mime. After some time, the teacher called their attention to a notice inviting them to attend an important meeting at the village hall — a building depicted in their design. In role as a government representative she informed them that because of the growth of population in a nearby city their village was to be flooded to make way for a reservoir. The children brought their acquired knowledge of water through previous topic work to the meeting. In this meeting their use of formal language was required by the dramatic context, and they gained confidence through speaking in role as the interested parties with hypotheses to present.

When the 'official' left the meeting, the discussion, and problem-solving strategies that they used were very sophisticated. Without teacher intervention they resolved the problem by publicizing their village as a place of historic interest. They took on the 'mantle of the expert', who knew what it was like to be threatened with relocation and how it would affect them. One child, in role as the village shopkeeper suggested that a museum be created, and each child, still in role, made appropriate contributions: a farmer produced an old plough, the village nurse found apothecaries bottles in her attic and one enterprising villager found Roman coins in her garden.

From this imagined experience many of the National Curriculum Programmes of Study were addressed – 'Speaking and Listening' in English, and also Programmes of Study in design technology and history. As Jonathan Neelands comments:

> In drama, the context is built on what is known by the group but it unfolds as a new story through the spontaneity of the dramatic interaction.
> (Neelands, 1992, p. 32)

What is interesting to note is that, in both classes, children with learning and physical difficulties were in no way disadvantaged. A hyperactive boy participating in the workhouse drama was absorbed in his role as the manager's 'trusty' and spent his time writing down occupations in a 'ledger' and shadowing the visitor to prevent the inmates from contact. In the 'flooded valley' drama the presence of a child restricted to a wheelchair focused attention upon special requirements in the village. She had chosen the role of village veterinarian and was instrumental in bringing the plight of farm animals, if flooding took place, to the attention of the meeting.

In these examples teachers were able to stimulate a wide range of learning activities across many areas of the curriculum. In particular it was noted that all the children, regardless of their ability, were motivated to discover more about their topic: they researched using textbooks and information technology, undertook creative writing, two- and three-dimensional artwork and composed music which they later utilized as a 'soundtrack' for an assembly presentation.

AFTERWORD

Throughout this chapter we have attempted to illustrate some of the ways in which drama is used in primary schools and to begin to identify theoretical perspectives on the art form's potency as a learning medium applicable to a wide range of situations and contexts, and accessible to all. We hope that teachers might use it as a resource from which to develop their own practice in this exciting curriculum area. In order that those interested in developing work in this area might do so we list some useful contacts and resources at the end of this book.

NOTES

[1] The theatre/drama divide has often been predicated on a narrow – and somewhat ethnocentric – conception of performance itself: the study of performance in other traditions clearly demonstrates that the clear separation of the role of audience from that of performer dominant in the West is by no means the only model available. Some of the alternative models of theatre practice extant are actually nearer to mainstream drama in education in form and function than they are to theatre as it is perceived

in the West. For a useful summary see Neelands (1994).
² Educators have come to regard drama as a 'spiral' rather than a 'linear' curriculum. A spiral curriculum model is characterized by concepts, skills and experiences continually being revisited throughout a child's development – but with increasing sophistication, complexity and degree of pupil autonomy. This is often contrasted with linear models, which tend to emphasize a 'building blocks' approach in which one concept builds upon – and relies upon – the previous one. There may be implications here for the suitability of the subject as an educational medium for children with special needs: this, and the fact that it is often claimed that drama is 'self-differentiating' (e.g. that differentiation is often by outcome, rather than by task), seems to imply that 'success' in drama is less dependent upon the possession of traditional logical-mathematical or linguistic 'intelligences' (Gardner, in Moon and Shelton Mayes, 1994, pp. 41–2).

REFERENCES

Boal, A. (1979) *Theatre of the Oppressed*. London: Pluto.
Bolton, G. (1979) *Towards a Theory of Drama in Education*. Harlow: Longman.
Department for Education (DFE) (1995) *Key Stages 1 and 2 of the National Curriculum*. London: HMSO.
Freire, P. (1972) *Pedagogy of the Oppressed*. London: Penguin.
HMI (1989) *Drama 5–16*. London: HMSO.
HMI (1990) *The Teaching and Learning of Drama*. London: HMSO.
Jackson, T. (ed.) (1993) *Learning Through Theatre*. London: Routledge.
Jennings, S. (1986) *Creative Drama in Groupwork*. Bicester: Winslow Press.
Johnson, L. and O'Neill, C. (eds) (1984) *Dorothy Heathcote: Collected Writings on Education and Drama*. London: Hutchinson.
Jones, E. and Reynolds, G. (1992) *The Play's the Thing – Teacher's Roles in Children's Play*. New York: Teachers College Press.
Moon, B. and Shelton Mayes, A. (1994) *Teaching and Learning in the Secondary School*. London: Routledge.
National Curriculum Council (NCC) (1990) *Drama in the National Curriculum* (poster). York: National Curriculum Council.
Neelands, J. (1984) *Making Sense of Drama*. Oxford: Heinemann.
Neelands, J. (1992) *Learning Through Imagined Experience*. London: Hodder & Stoughton.
Neelands, J. (1994) Theatre Without Walls, *Drama – The Journal of National Drama*, 2 (2), pp. 6–14.
Nicholson, H. (1994) Drama and the arts – from polemic to practice – celebrating ourselves as experts, *Drama – The Journal of National Drama*, 3 (1).
O'Toole, J. (1992) *The Process of Drama*. London: Routledge.
Peter, M. (1994) *Drama for All – Developing Drama in the Curriculum with Pupils with Special Educational Needs*. London: David Fulton.
Rainer, J. (ed.) (1989) *The Arts in Schools Project – Drama*. Wigan: Wigan MBC Education Department.
Somers, J. (1994) *Drama in the Curriculum*. London: Cassell.
Wagner, B.J. (1977) *Drama as a Learning Medium*. London: Hutchinson.

—4—

An ear for music

Anthony Walker

The purpose of this chapter is not to investigate various designations of special needs in depth, but rather to offer suggestions based on good music practice and National Curriculum requirements. It should assist you in promoting the musical abilities and interests of your children with special needs.

Music is for all our children, assisting their personal and social development and enriching their lives. Together with the other fine arts it marks out differences between merely existing and truly living, reaching beyond material needs into a mysterious, rewarding and fulfilling world of beauty.

All our children can be helped to learn to enjoy and to become involved in music to some extent. Music can be of inestimable value for children who have difficulties in hearing, seeing, moving, thinking or responding. A single instrument, even one as simple as a tambour or shaker, can possess qualities of sound and tone irresistible enough to reach a child in a direct, uncomplicated manner. Children who experience severe obstacles in forming relationships with other children, adults and their environment can achieve security and joy in making music. By means of music, we can assist these children to come to maturity in many ways.

Music ought to be:

- an essential part of the education of all our children
- concerned with performing, composing and listening
- developing skills, sensitivity and understanding
- fun and enjoyable for pupils and teachers.

In addition to having its own conceptual framework (e.g. rhythm, pitch and timbre) and its unique forms of expression (e.g. singing and playing percussion instruments) music confers non-musical benefits that have particular consequences for pupils with special needs. It contributes to:

- reasoning ability
- language development

- reading skills
- feelings and response
- socializing and pleasurable experiences in a group
- personal fulfilment
- motor control and physical well-being
- positive attitudes to school
- the promotion of communication.

Music is one of the few subject areas in which the child with special needs can be integrated into the class. Full use ought to be made of each child's music potential. Listening can help a child to overcome – at least for a time – difficulties or pain by relaxing.

For all our pupils, fundamental music experiences and patterns of learning are the same. It is in the scope and rate of learning that differences are revealed. Blind children are not able to read music notation; they can, however, be taught Braille notation. Children who are not able to walk cannot move or dance to music; they can, however, be taught to keep time, respond and express themselves in other ways, perhaps by hand or arm movements. Pupils with severe learning difficulties may not be able to grasp music concepts but can be taught to share in musical experiences. Those with exceptional musical gifts can be encouraged to promote their skills further by joining in local choirs or more advanced group music-making.

NATIONAL CURRICULUM MUSIC

Under National Curriculum Orders, all pupils, including those with special needs, should have the opportunity of taking part in music. The proposals reviewing the music curriculum, published in May 1994, pointed to a reduction in the statutory content:

> The overall aim of the changes to the music Order is to clarify the essential skills, knowledge and understanding which should be taught, whilst safeguarding the breadth of the curriculum.
>
> (DFE, 1994b, p. ii)

There are two Attainment Targets (ATs) in England:

- AT1 Performing and Composing
- AT2 Listening and Appraising

The ATs are shown by the End of Key Stage Descriptors (EKSDs) for Music, pointing to the nature and span of performance which the majority of pupils should exhibit by the end of a Key Stage.

There are six parts to the Programmes of Study (PoS):

1. A statement of the musical opportunities that should be given to pupils.
2. Pupils should be taught, in all musical activities, to listen with concentration, to explore and to internalize. The musical elements that they should be able to recognize, including their use within the structure of music, are: pitch; duration; tempo; timbre; texture.
3. Notes on the repertoire for performing and listening.
4. The musical opportunities, common to each Key Stage, to be given to pupils. These opportunities are:
   AT1
   • control of sounds
   • performing with others
   • composing
   • communicating musical ideas to others
   AT2
   • listening to, and developing understanding of music from different times and cultures
   • responding to and evaluating music.
5. An outline of the activities that pupils should be taught for AT1.
6. An outline of the activities that pupils should be taught for AT2.

There are no Standard Attainment Tests (SATs) in music. The EKSDs are devised to help teachers judge how their pupils' attainment in Performing and Composing, Listening and Appraising meets expectations. Assessment should be continuous and founded on the teacher's observations. The new Orders, circulated to schools in January 1995, came into effect on 1 August 1995.

Note the measures taken to increase access to National Curriculum Music for all pupils:

1. Key Stage PoS are written in such a way that each has elements that can be taught to all pupils in ways appropriate to their abilities.
2. Provision is made at each Key Stage for those pupils at each end of the ability range to work from earlier or later Programmes of Study.

SCHOOLS. It is necessary for schools to make suitable provision for pupils requiring:

• alternative means of communication to that of speech
• non-sighted methods of reading
• musical instruments that are specially adapted for handling and playing
• technological aids such as computer equipment, software and keyboards

- musical instruments that transmit strong vibrations
- aids that allow access to music inside and outside school.

TEACHERS. Teachers should be able to:

- identify the wide range of demands of pupils, from those with special difficulties to those who are specially gifted in music
- analyse the problems and provide practical assistance for some children and present challenges and wide opportunities for others
- ensure that all pupils can view their work in music in a progressive way, building on past skills and achievements
- consider planning, teaching, assessing and the provision of musical resources in a thoughtful and sensitive manner
- integrate the work of pupils with special needs into general classroom activities in music.

No pupil should be excluded from National Curriculum music. Indeed, music has special characteristics being:

- a source of delight
- a means of gaining fulfilment in successful achievement
- an agency to assist learning in other curricular areas.

We would be prudent to select the learning activities from the PoS which will allow our pupils to experience a developing sense of personal worth, growth in confidence, definite and positive individual contributions to music and a response to the music of others.

PUPILS. The National Curriculum Council (1993) defined four categories of pupils with special needs. These groups are listed below, with suggestions for approaches to the music curriculum:

1. Pupils with exceptionally severe learning difficulties.
2. Pupils with other learning difficulties.
3. Pupils with physical or sensory impairment.
4. Pupils who are exceptionally able.

Pupils with learning difficulties

In the ordinary classroom the children in groups one and two learn more slowly and in smaller degrees than their peers. With short attention spans and limited linguistic skills, they require plenty of repetitional work. Books or written music notation are of little help to them. They can, however, be attentive and receptive to music, in which they are often able to do a variety of things.

Two kinds of songs are essential:

- songs with much repetition of words and music
- songs incorporating active involvement.

The elements of repetition and action in songs can help in bringing pupils to focus on the words. It may be necessary to change the songs and activities frequently. Help can be given by the teacher singing the children's names to them, or inserting a child's name into the words of a song. Body awareness, feelings of identity and self-esteem can be developed by songs naming parts of the body.

It requires very little technical know-how from primary teachers willing to sing with the children, thereby extending and developing the child's innate interest and joy in singing. All children have the right to sing. The aim should be to engage in a joyful, creative, spiritual and emotional act of sharing rather than a striving towards note-accuracy and forced performance.

Singing without words (using 'lah', humming or a vowel sound) can be of special benefit to children with learning difficulties. Echo and copying games, question and answer, call and respond, with their emphasis on free improvising and absence of tunes or words to remember, have great benefits. Many children will need to be reminded of right and left sides of the body or the progression of movements in action songs and other musical activities.

Music can be of great benefit to autistic, introverted and unsociable children. With its distinctive nature it can summon up an aura very unlike the 'normal' classroom situation that many agitated children may find threatening and thwarting. Singing, moving, playing instruments and joining in with others reveals music's powerful social stimulus.

Songs with words that promote sensitivity to others in a social setting are important. Clear directions during singing and playing, together with orderly procedures in giving out and collecting instruments, can assist children with emotional difficulties to follow directions and point to the necessity for care and courtesy. Sometimes humming or singing to 'lah' will prove to be of benefit to pupils with speech and language impairments.

Modified music notation, by the employment of colours, signs, letters and symbols, can greatly assist pupils with learning difficulties. The system of colour-coding of notes, pioneered by John Raymond Tobin (1886–1967), has resulted in various publications to assist in learning to play the recorder, guitar and piano.

The raw materials of music (single notes, rhythms, pulse, accent, intervals, chords and timbre) are part of a living procedure, releasing a potent effect on the emotional life and assisting the integration of the maturing individual child.

Pupils with physical or sensory impairment

For the children in group three – those with physical or sensory impairment – physical activity in music can be modified to assist children who may be limited in mobility or lack control of motor skills. Children in wheelchairs can take part in movement or dancing to music by moving their arms or upper bodies rhythmically. Body sounds can take place in different ways: foot-tapping on the floor, tapping on a table or desktop, thigh-slapping, waist-clapping, flicking the fingers and so on. Pupils can be encouraged to invent their own movements, suited to their disability, and expressing the music. In group activities, dependable classmates can take turns to help those who are unable to walk.

Stands specially made to hold or support instruments such as recorders, melodicas and guiros can free a hand to read Braille or to assist the child with one arm. Instruments such as cymbals, drums and xylophone can be played by foot attachments. Special grips on beaters, large handles or holders on percussion instruments and double-headed beaters can help those with problems of grasping. Appendix A of Bailey's pioneering volume (1973) gives full details and sketches of comprehensive, imaginative gadgetry. It also has a comprehensive bibliography.

The circumstance of pupils with impaired sight causes them to listen assiduously and to recall what they hear. They can do very well in the music class and contribute to the general skills in imitating words and phrases. Songs that include simulations of animal and bird sounds, wind, thunder, rain, hail, whistles, rattles and traffic are essential to the development of a response to sounds around us. Songbooks published by A & C Black provide varied and stimulating material.

A photocopying machine with the power of enlarging script from the original is an essential to assist pupils with impaired vision. Unlike their sighted friends, blind pupils cannot be helped towards reading music at sight. Working out Braille notation is a difficult and time-consuming task. It is wise to arrange for vision-impaired children to practise music beforehand on their own so that they have advanced preparation.

Moving to music, with its risk of physical injury and possibly unfamiliar surroundings, can be very trying. A sighted child can, of course, assist in moving round the area. Very definite and clear directions are essential for any moving to music activities. When instruments are used the children should be encouraged to identify them by touch as well as by sound.

As they sing mostly by rote, these pupils do need very clear directions from the teacher, but fine diction for the children to copy and clear pronunciation of the words are necessary. They need to listen hard and you need to articulate well.

Although most sounds are passed to the brain via the ears,

vibrations can be experienced through the rest of the body. The sense of touch can greatly assist the ear. Pupils with hearing impairment should be encouraged to touch all manner of sound sources, especially those with strong vibrations. Large drums and bells, bass resonator bars, metallophones, cello, double-bass and pedal notes on the organ should be experienced.

Generally, the emphasis on mouth shapes and sounds in singing can assist the child with hearing and speech difficulties to be more sensitive to the language of speech. The talking drum idea from Africa can be a help; short and simple phrases of words are played on drums of different sizes. Rhymes, chants, contrasts between high and low, fast and slow can assist in languge development. The beginnings of songs, drama with music, movement to music and listening music can be indicated by visual symbols as well as the spoken voice. Taking part in music sessions can provide a unique sense of repose as well as promoting self-confidence in bodily movements and developing social links with other pupils.

Hand signs connected with the music-teaching methods of John Curwen (1816–80) and Zoltán Kodály (1882–1967) can assist the visual perception of music. The teacher's employment of hand movements indicating levels of pitch, establishing a connection between sounds and symbols, gives positive initial help.

Singing can be of much support in helping communication disorders such as stuttering, stammering, weak articulation, incorrect sequences of words, affected pitch range and irregularities of the voice. Fluency and control are improved by the sustaining of vowels, movement of rhythm and repetition of words in vocal music. Copying games, question and answer games, echo music and the singing of children's names (perhaps in the form of a class register) can all promote the children's learning in music.

Pupils who are exceptionally able

It is our duty as teachers to ensure that the fourth group of children with special needs – the exceptionally able – make progress at their exceptional rate through National Curriculum music and that they are receiving enriching musical experiences with the National Curriculum Programmes of Study. Support services in music, which formerly did so much to assist the development of these pupils, are now at risk owing to the changing role of Local Education Authorities (LEAs).

It is essential to look at possibilities for broadening and extending the skills, understanding and knowledge of able pupils. The following includes some of the music services which it would be wise to investigate:

- post-school or Saturday morning classes organized by local colleges or education authorities. The national music colleges offer specialist training for gifted children in their junior departments. Entrance is by audition and financial help may be available
- weekend or short courses. Many of these are advertised in the monthly journal *The Music Teacher*
- instrumental or vocal lessons, many of which are offered by LEAs
- choirs and orchestras, instrumental groups and workshops for young people.

There are five specialist music schools taking children from the junior age range in Britain at the time of writing. Scholarships are available for children who show exceptional promise. They are Chetham's School of Music, Manchester; The Yehudi Menuhin School, Cobham; The Purcell School, Harrow on the Hill; Wells Cathedral School, Somerset and – the newest of all – St Mary's Music School, Edinburgh. Details of their courses and admission procedures can be obtained direct from the institution; full addresses can be found in education and music yearbooks, and directories in your local library.

INFORMATION TECHNOLOGY

The utilization of information technology and electronic equipment in the primary classroom has given a new impulse to music education. Obstacles encountered by pupils with special needs have in many cases been surmounted. Practical activities of composing, performing and listening are promoted by pupils of wide abilities participating at their own level. Touch screens, touch switches and Braille keyboards allow pupils with varying problems to have access to information technology, enhancing their appreciation of the properties of sound.

Computers and electronic keyboards are the items most frequently to be found in the primary classroom. Computer programmes allow pupils to select, organize, change and create sounds, and to retain them for retrieval at a future date. There are many kinds of electronic keyboards, enabling pupils to do differentiated tasks and produce thoughtful compositions. Sounds can be synthesized, changed and preserved. Information technology is an extra resource which needs to form part of a broad, balanced curriculum in music. Care should be taken over the placing of all electronic equipment so that all pupils can gain access with ease, and avoid dangers of trailing leads, awkwardly placed sockets and loose plugs and connections. One great advantage is that pupils don't have to gather others together to perform their music: the results can be heard immediately.

Previously, only pupils with keyboard skills could aspire to electronic music-making. Further, many of these pupils cannot manipulate the beating, blowing, pressing and striking required on conventional instruments. Lacking fine movements, control of breath, fingers, eyes and ears meant that musical involvement with others was almost impossible. A radical advance in music technology is 'Soundbeam', launched in 1990, which allows physical movements, including small gesticulations, to produce musical sounds. Giving forth an ultrasonic beam, it detects the existence of anything in its path, transforming the details of distance and movement into MIDI data, an electronic code that can send instructions to electronic instruments. Pupils with hearing impairment can feel their music through 'Soundbox' or the larger 'Soundbed'. Group music performances can be created and all pupils – with disabilities or not – can experience the joy of making music together.

Music should help all of our pupils in their everyday living. It is easy to attract and hold the attention through music; our teaching should be planned so that every child can respond fully to music at his or her own level. Many able children will learn to play an instrument to a high standard and learn to read music fluently. The world of music includes several personalities, such as the violinist Itzhak Perlman, the pianist Stevie Wonder, the percussionist Evelyn Glennie and the conductor Jeffrey Tate who, despite severe disabilities, have attained the pinnacles of the profession. Your children with special needs may be unable to achieve these things but this should not bar them from learning, taking part and finding fulfilment in the power and beauty of music.

REFERENCES

Bailey, P. (1973) *They Can Make Music*. London: Oxford University Press.
Department for Education (DFE) (1994a) *Music for Ages 5–14: Revised orders*. London: HMSO.
Department for Education (DFE) (1994b) *Music in the National Curriculum: Draft Proposals*. London: HMSO.
National Curriculum Council (NCC) (1993) *Music 5–14*. London: NCC.

Black songbooks:

Appuskidu (1975). London: A & C Black.
Carol, Gaily Carol (1973). London: A & C Black.
Okki Tokki Unga (1976). London: A & C Black.

FURTHER READING

At the time of writing there are many texts, songbooks, instrumental tutors and coursebooks for the class teacher in music. The field of music for children with special needs, however, is far less well documented.

The 1970s and early 1980s witnessed the publication of invaluable, pioneering texts on the value, role and practice of music in special education. Teachers' books and songbooks by P. Nordoff and C. Robbins rapidly gained classic status. They include:
(1971) *Therapy in Music for Handicapped Children*. London: Gollancz.
(1975) *Music Therapy in Special Education*. London: Macdonald and Evans.
(1977) *Creative Music Therapy: Individualised Treatment for the Handicapped Child*. New York: John Day.

Likewise, Juliette Alvin's books were leading texts:
(1976) *Music for the Handicapped Child*, 2nd edn. London: OUP.
(1978) *Music Therapy for the Autistic Child*. London: OUP.
The 1978 publication – the only book of its kind on the subject was reissued by OUP in 1991 under the title *Music Therapy for the Handicapped Child*. It has three additional chapters by Auriel Warwick founded on her recent research and describing case-study material.

David Ward, Principal Officer of the Dartington Music Foundation for the Handicapped, wrote two influential books based on his wide experience with young people:
(1976) *Hearts and Hands and Voices: Music in the Education of Slow Learners*. Oxford: Oxford University Press.
(1979) *Sing a Rainbow: Musical Activities with Mentally Handicapped Children*. Oxford: Oxford University Press.

In the early 1980s Audrey Wisbey produced two books based on her work on children with learning problems:
(1980) *Music as the Source of Learning*. Lancaster: Music Therapists Publications.
(1981) *Learn to Sing to Learn to Read: A Course Book for Parents and Teachers*. London: BBC.
Among other influential publications from the 1970s and 1980s were:
Dickinson, P.I. (1976) *Music with ESN Children: A Guide for the Classroom Teacher*. Windsor: National Foundation for Educational Research.
Dobbs, J.P.B. (1966) *The Slow Learner and Music: A Handbook for Teachers*. London: OUP.
Orff, G. (1980) *The Orff Music Therapy*. London: Schott.
Wood, M. (1983) *Music for Mentally Handicapped People*. London: Souvenir Press.
Invaluable to the non-musician wishing to organize music activities, this book has been reissued in 1993 under the title *Music for People with Learning Disabilities*.

Recently there has been a resurgence of interest in publishing in this field. For example:

Bean, J. and Oldfield, A. (1991) *Pied Piper: Musical Activities to Develop Basic Skills*. Cambridge: Cambridge University Press. Eighty musical activities designed for those with a wide variety of special needs. A valuable resource book for teachers with no specialist musical background.

Heal, M. and Wigram, T. (eds) (1993) *Music Therapy in Health and Education*. London: Jessica Kingsley. Based on papers from a 1992 Cambridge conference held under the auspices of the British Society for Music Therapy and the Association of Professional Music Therapists, it includes contributors from eight countries.

Ockleford, A. (1993) *Music and Visually Impaired Children: Some Notes for the Guidance of Teachers*. London: Royal National Institute for the Blind. A booklet written by the Head of Music at a school for visually impaired children.

Streeter, E. (1993) *Making Music with the Young Child with Special Needs*. London: Jessica Kingsley. A guide for primary school teachers.

RNIB (1992) *Braille Music Primer – Part One*. London: Royal National Institute for the Blind. The braille music system is explained in this introductory guide.

Other publications:

Addison, R. (1993) *Bright Ideas: Music*. Leamington Spa: Scholastic Publications.

Gilbert, J. (1989) *Musical Starting-Points with Young Children*. East Grinstead: Ward Lock Educational.

York, M. (1988) *Gently into Music: Possible Approaches for Non-specialist Primary Teachers*. Harlow: Longman.

-5
Oracy and SEN

Rita Ray

When National Curriculum recognized the importance of talk for learning, teachers felt that oracy had been given its rightful place and that here at least was one subject they could feel confident with. Yet, as a subject to plan, monitor and assess, Speaking and Listening is wide ranging and hard to pin down. The development of language underlies the whole curriculum. The Programme of Study states that primary pupils should be taught to:

- use the vocabulary and grammar of spoken standard English
- formulate, clarify and express their ideas
- adapt their speech to a widening range of circumstances and demands
- listen, understand and respond appropriately to others.

Within this framework teachers must plan for children's individual needs and create opportunities for talk to develop learning and to make all children's achievements explicit, including those who have special educational needs. Rather than using official technical terms to define what is meant by special educational needs I shall quote a summary of features arrived at by a group of teachers:

Pupils with special educational needs have been described variously as pupils:

- who need help in making links in learning, who have specific blocks in their progress which they need help to overcome;
- who have physical or sensory disabilities;
- who pick up and remember things more quickly than others;
- who are consistently disruptive of the learning of others;
- who have difficulty in relating to others, perhaps because of aspects of personality, or because of past or present experience;
- who need more time and reinforcement to arrive at understanding;
- who frequently become marginalized, remaining on the periphery of learning activities;
- who are perceived by the teacher or the school as having particular learning difficulties;

- who consistently remain quiet, or persistently seek to dominate others.

The teachers arrived at a practical, working principle:

> A pupil may be considered to have special educational needs when the level of his/her learning is giving cause for concern. When this happens, a teacher needs to consider the particular pupil, the other pupils, the classroom provision, the role of the teacher and the school.

In what follows I shall attempt to discuss current ideas about spoken language in school, relate it to the classroom situation and suggest practical courses of action in developing and assessing spoken language. As the teachers' summary showed there are several reasons why a child might need special help with language. The reasons may be divided into two main categories – physical and environmental. I shall look at both categories, bearing in mind that whatever the reasons may be, the same requirement, for systematic, individual planning within the class context, applies. As emphasized in National Curriculum documents, all pupils have a right to have their individual needs provided for within the context of a shared curricular experience.

Some children receive extra help from support staff. In the case of those who do not, the teacher has to accommodate their needs in class planning. This means placing children in suitable groups for different purposes in order to raise or maintain particular children's competence. The teacher has to make judgements on the basis of the cognitive demands of the task, the readiness of the individual and the mix of personalities of the children who are to work together – which ones will dominate, which ones might be swamped.

The Code of Practice (1994) for children with special educational needs guides teachers through the stages of assessing special educational needs within their school and classroom and delineates the types of provision appropriate for these needs.

HOME IS WHERE THE START IS?

> My kid, he too scared to talk 'cause nobody play by the rules he know. At home I can't shut him up.
>
> (Heath, 1982, p. 107)

> I don't like to blame the parents – they try very hard – but we do get them straight from home, so what else can we blame it on?
> (Teacher quoted in Early Years Language Project, University of Exeter)

The understanding and use of language is the basis of learning. Articles and research about children's language pinpoint two main reasons for linguistic deficiency – developmental delay and social class. The social class deficit model is constantly challenged (e.g., Wells, 1987; Tizard and Hughes, 1994). The report of the Bristol University research project directed by Gordon Wells claimed that intensive monitoring of children's language at home and at school showed 'significant social class differences in children's language development'. The difficulties some working-class children have are attributed to a lack of knowledge of books and stories as a means of acquiring 'symbolic language'. Wells's solution is for schools to engender 'the essential knowledge of books and stories' to compensate. Wells asserted that teachers' higher assessment of children who had a more literate background was due to the fact that these children understood the teachers' use of language. The child had to pay attention to the literate form of language used by the teacher and be able to reconstruct meaning. 'Our study had working class children whose command of language was advanced and superb, but who lacked the ability to handle ideas using the symbolic potential of language' (Wells, 1984).

Teachers work hard on bridging the gap between home and school in the ways recommended by researchers such as Wells. Many of the home–school factors he identifies are practical, such as, 'The first and most obvious cause of the impoverished interaction that so often occurs between teachers and pupils is the number of children involved – 30 or more in the average class'. The conversations children have with carers at home are long, with points explained, whereas in class discussions children compete for the teacher's time and attention. Children may contribute single comments which cannot be followed up and they cannot concentrate on listening when they are looking for an opportunity to speak.

Daniels and Lee (1989) argue that Wells' work can be interpreted in a different way: 'Wells appears to be measuring success in the education system by the attributes/achievements of those who succeed in the education system . . . a self-fulfilling prophecy'.

Tizard and Hughes (1984) concentrate on the discontinuity between working-class homes and nursery schools and identify some deficiencies in the school rather than in the home. They put forward four main areas of mismatch:

1. Teachers pose a series of questions rather than fostering conversations like the ones that occur at home.
2. The kind of 'play' set up in school differs considerably from the 'learning context and everyday living' of the children's homes.
3. The negative evaluation of working-class children's language and classroom behaviour resulted in teachers 'lowering their expectations and standards for the working class children'.

4. Teachers underestimate children's abilities and interests because they hold certain beliefs about the children's home background, such as 'working class children do nothing at home except watch TV'.

Michaels (1981) asserts that school linguistic demands are at variance with *all* homes. The teacher's notion of sharing a story, for example, is far removed from everyday conversational accounts. Everything must be named and described, even when they are in plain sight and minimal shared background should be assumed.

How many researchers have a working-class background themselves or talk to teachers and parents who have a working-class background? Does working-class background matter at all or is the term 'working class' simply a convenient way for researchers to describe language that does not go down well in school? Most teachers from a working-class background will recognize the 'bilingual' approach necessary between home and school. It has been well documented by poets and novelists. A direct and vivid example is the following extract from a poem by Liz Lochhead, illustrating the difference between home dialect and standard English. The home dialect is inextricably linked with family and to criticize the dialect can be to criticize those who use it:

> It was January and a guy dreek day
> the first day I went to school
> so ma mum happ'd me up
> in ma guid navy blue nap coat
> with the red tartan hood
> burl'd a scarf around ma neck
> poo'd on ma pixie and ma pockies
> it was that bitter

Is it not time for the home/playground/school language debate to be resolved? Most teachers adopt a balanced and intelligent approach, valuing the children's language, indeed, being pleased at any small steps in development where some children are concerned. The dilemma often occurs for most of us when children begin to write. There is no question about introducing all children to standard English since not to do so would be to hinder their progress and opportunities. It is hard to separate standard English and ideas of élitism. It is noticeable that, especially in England rather than in other UK countries, festivals of drama, poetry and literature at school level are usually the domain of those who 'speak properly'. There is a great deal more at stake here than simply the way we pronounce words. Daniels and Lee (1989, p. 42) conclude:

> it is not that middle class knowledge, discourse, understanding,

meaning are cognitively and intellectually superior to that of the working classes but that their versions of the stories are perceived as the legitimate versions within the present social context of schooling.

INDIVIDUAL DIFFERENCES – THERE'S MORE TO LANGUAGE THAN WORDS

Where children have language/speech problems associated with conditions such as autism, hearing impairment, Down's syndrome and so on, specialist help is needed to explain their difficulties to the school and help to plan programmes for them. Teachers should not be afraid to involve such children and to expect them to join in. Having a specific condition does not alter a child's basic humanity and need to be initiated into the normal activities of childhood. The teacher can feel confident that he or she can fulfil the child's most important need – to develop as a person. Provided a child is not so disruptive as to interfere with the education of others it is better to be in a mainstream class where the peer group can do far more, formally and informally, for a child's development than hours of adult intervention.

There is more to the perception of language than words. For a project, I asked teachers to choose a group of children with low (40–50) IQ scores. From the chosen group they assured me that Peter had the best command of language while Carl had the worst. Other adults, welfare workers, nursery nurses and classroom assistants confirmed this view. 'Language ability' seems to indicate a willingness to communicate combined with pleasant facial expressions. Peter was a good example of this. He supplemented his speech with intonation, gesture and expression to get his meaning over. Carl was a solemn, rigid child who spoke in a monotone, hardly changed his anxious expression and made no discernible gestures. When the transcripts of their speech were 'scored' Carl had used the most complex speech in the group and Peter had used the least complex. Peter was much easier to listen to, which gave an impression of good language attainment. Here are typical 20-word samples from each child's transcript.

> Peter: (talking about a jigsaw) Look ... more ... more elephant ... there ... there ... go there ... go there ... go there ... cow ... oh horns ... bull ... there ... cow ... elephant ... cow.

> Carl: Joanne and Linda haven't come today. Joanne's gone to the doctor's, Linda's gone to the nurse, gone to see them.

Peter said 'go there' eight times – four times as a statement, twice in a questioning tone, once in a puzzled tone when he was sure the jigsaw piece should really fit, and once in a conclusive, satisfied tone as he clicked in the last bit of a section. So we could translate Peter's 'go there' as:

It goes there. (four times)
Does it go there? (twice)
It should go there but it doesn't. (once)
It goes there and I've finished. (once)

Sometimes children who have learning difficulties can use language in a directive way to talk themselves through a task. A child with visual and co-ordination problems could talk herself through, e.g., putting together a jigsaw. Although she had problems organizing the task she could say, 'Head goes at top, feet go at bottom' etc. Without her own commentary she could not do the task.

Talking, working, playing and taking part in activity-based learning with other children can raise the attainment level of a child with special needs. The kind of group the child works in – friendship group, attainment group, pair – depends on the nature of the activity. In tasks which rely on prior skill and knowledge it is important to place the child with children working at or just above his or her level so that it is possible to make the cognitive shift to the next stage. Children with special needs may stay at one stage for longer than other children and move gradually rather than making sudden leaps forward.

Standard English

We should not confuse élitism with the pursuit of excellence, which is open to all. In practical terms, how should the switch from speech to written, standard English be approached sensitively? We should acknowledge the history and validity of dialect and have some insight into its origins. For example, the area of Wigan in Lancashire has a rich dialect and quick decisions are needed when children are at the stage of trying to write spoken language. One child, at the stage of writing letters from his own name and beginning to associate some sound relationships asked how to spell 'fet' . 'Say the whole thing for me, Robert.' 'My dragon is big and if you see him you have fet run very fast.' Here is an old English construction still used in Wigan. In full it reads, 'you have for to run very fast', as in the old rhyme, 'Simple Simon went a-fishing, *for to* catch a whale'. At Robert's stage I would reproduce his language phonetically and write 'fet'. When Robert has read more, been read to more and moved to the next stage of writing, I might consider discussing an alternative to 'fet' in written work, making explicit the difference between spoken and written language.

Children understand differences in the way people speak to one another from their own experience. One way to tap this is to set up role-play with opportunities to use different registers, e.g., an accident. Children have to describe the accident they have seen to:

- a friend
- a carer
- a doctor
- the police.

It is surprising how early children pick up on the appropriateness of different ways of speaking for different situations. In the 'accident' role-play children usually adopt a more formal tone when reporting to the police and the doctor. In free play children demonstrate that they have picked up a lot about the different ways people speak and behave. Listening to children in play situations tells us much about this.

Anyone who has observed children playing in the 'home corner' will have been struck by the stereotypical nature of young children's spontaneous play. Rather than reflecting real home situations the home corner seems to have a self-perpetuating culture removed from the real world. Children of new men and househusbands persist in the notion that mother always does the chores and father goes out to work. This is even more marked if they are improvising traditional stories in which sexism prevails, as this extract from a Reception 'café' set-up demonstrates (in fact the story they are using, *The Hungry Giant*, is not sexist but they have other giant stories in mind):

Rachel, Sarah, John and Christopher are just starting to play. The girls are preparing 'food'. J and C sit at the table. C taps a plastic knife on the table.

C: I WANT MY DINNER.
S: There you are – nice peas.
R: Nice peas.
R: Shall I put more on?
J: Oh right.
C: You've got more than me.
S: We're going out together (S and R). Bye. Are you coming after you've finished?
J: Are we, are we?
C: We're giants. We change into giants . . . I'm going to get a little boy and cut him in half, OK?
S: Giant, you want a little bit more?
R: Has anyone got a plate?
C: Yum, yum. I haven't got a plate. I want a big plate for a big dinner. (To J) Do you want a big dinner? (S and R rush to replace small plates with big ones) Right, there's a big plate.
R: It's done now, it's done now. (S brings more food)

C: Fee fi fo fum, I can smell the blood of an Englishman. Bring me some honey or I'll hit you with my bommy knocker.
S: Here's some honey.
C: (To J) Ask her for some honey.
S: We're going out to work now. You be our husbands.
C: Yeah, but we're giants. You be giants' wives. Girls can't be giants 'cause girls don't eat people. (To J) We're going out to work to kill people, aren't we?

When teachers are asked where these ideas about male and female roles come from they usually attribute them to traditional stories and television advertisements. So, although we are urged to introduce traditional stories and rhymes at home, teachers then have to set about remedying the attitudes engendered. This is usually attempted through the promotion of equal opportunities in everyday class situations and by reading 'antidote' stories such as *The Practical Princess*.

The planning and setting up of play situations is a vital component in the development of language for learning. Some good examples of this kind of planning are demonstrated on a videotape, *Structured Play at Key Stage 1*.[1] The teachers plan and show in action several cross-curricular play situations. One feature of the play is the logical way in which it is linked to recording and literacy skills. The teacher reflects on the play with the children and extracts points that were planned into the play. For example, after play sessions in a cake shop the teacher, in a carpet discussion, asks one group to tell the class how many doughnuts they sold, how many buns, etc. On a small table the teacher piles up different coloured large cubes for each kind of cake. There appears a simple three-dimensional block graph as the children report what they sold. For that session it had been planned to introduce the concept of recording in this way through the cake shop play.

In planning and discussing, teachers had looked at the introduction of English, maths and science concepts and skills through play in a structured way. The play environments are available for spontaneous, creative play as well. Further planning of this kind was applied to looking at what to expect of a play situation at different year levels and how progression can be built into play. A hospital/doctor's surgery set-up becomes more elaborate as it is considered in the context of Reception to Year 2 and beyond. From Year 2 onwards, for example, there are opportunities to measure weight, height and temperature using appropriate instruments. There is also a receptionist's desk with appointments book and alphabetical card index records. This kind of play situation can be extended logically into more complex activity-based learning for Key Stage 2 pupils. The planning has specific aims and targets as well as allowing for flexible creative play. In these contexts key concepts and their accompanying language can be introduced at all levels in a way that is appropriate for all children.

So far as using play and activity-based learning to develop language is concerned it is recognized that new linguistic structures are more readily learned and retained in active rather than passive situations. Lawrence Leonard also recommended the occasional involvement of an adult role-player to lead the play and to bring the desired language structures and vocabulary into the context.

The role of adults in oracy needs to be considered carefully. How many teachers have felt that they have just taken part in a satisfying talk session with young children only to discover (if they left a tape running) that teacher did 90 per cent of the talking and most of that was asking questions? I certainly have. Tizard and Wells point out the importance of creating a conversational framework rather than interrogating the children, of starting up a conversation about a class story just read rather than focusing on questioning children. Labov, in his seminal research on non-standard English (1972) showed how a child in an 'interview' situation with a teacher could be assessed as monosyllabic and language delayed. In a different situation, i.e., with a teacher from his own neighbourhood background, sitting informally with a friend and a focus for conversation, the child spoke in sentences and demonstrated understanding he would not otherwise have been credited with.

MULTILINGUAL DIVERSITY

In a more specific learning situation than the one described by Labov, Varkalis (1991) describes how children's drawings improved when the lesson was conducted in their home language. As Wittgenstein (1961) remarked, 'What belongs to language is a whole culture'. The children working with Varkalis were 'given permission' to bring their language and therefore their culture into the classroom, enriching the outcomes of the lesson.

Linguistic diversity is still occasionally viewed as a problem. It is an accomplishment to speak more than one language and it is amazing that so many young children manage it rather well. Any problems usually arise from social or cultural sources, rather than purely linguistic ones – though Wittgenstein implies that there are no purely linguistic issues. They all have a cultural element. Children are often shy about using their home language in school. Sometimes the conflict is such that a child will just stop talking for a while. They might also have been advised by parents according to their own school experience under a different system, where respect, obedience and silence were demanded, so the child is receiving conflicting messages.

Bilingualism is sometimes blamed for other difficulties or special needs a child may have. Teachers want to give the benefit of the doubt and try to cope for as long as possible to give the child a fair chance. Even children with severe difficulties can tune in to the use of home language or second language at the right time and can often manage some speech at their own level in both languages. It is important not to draw conclusions from one case and to avoid stereotyping, otherwise expectations may be lowered and the child's attainment level depressed.

The use and highlighting of home language depends too on the number of children in a school who speak the language. A single child in a class can feel embarrassed and conspicuous at the most well meaning attempts to acknowledge his or her home language. Teachers need to draw upon knowledge and experience to decide how to deal with each situation.

USING TAPE RECORDERS

Tape recorders can enhance all children's language facility. A recording and listening area or 'Talk Box' can be a permanent feature in the classroom. It can also be used with a junction box and a set of headphones for listening to stories and other material. The tape recorder can be used to:

- retell stories
- give instructions for making something, test the instructions on a partner and modify
- describe events in personal life
- record science observations
- record topic material, tables, etc., for those who learn better through auditory modality
- make a tape of poetry, jokes for a class tape library.

I have observed children listening to and reflecting on their own talk to advantage – e.g., a child with indistinct speech practised, of his own accord, with the tape recorder and made improvements that speech therapy had been unable to achieve because of his self-consciousness in practising with a therapist; a girl of nine who was still at the stage of making grammatical errors such as 'comed' and 'drawed' was able to move herself on as she listened to herself on tape and noticed her own errors.

Children love listening to themselves and feel that their language is valued if others listen. When tape recorders are introduced children will spend some time playing and exploring before they gain confidence but, once tape recorders are part of the normal school day, the children will learn how to organize themselves to make best use of them.

ASSESSING SPOKEN LANGUAGE

How can teachers judge the level at which a child is working in Speaking and Listening? Children are expected, for example, to 'listen to others and respond appropriately' and to 'use some of the core features of standard English vocabulary and grammar appropriately'. If teachers were not told that the former requirement is for Level 1 and the latter for Level 4 it would not be immediately apparent. There are no specific indicators of what is meant by listening and responding appropriately within Level 1 or which core features of standard English are appropriate within Level 4. Even if samples are produced and agreed upon for a particular school or group of schools the countrywide standards across England and Wales cannot be assured. Speaking and Listening also has some of the most wide-ranging, spontaneous and fugitive outcomes to be captured and assessed.

Where children with special educational needs are concerned the teacher has the challenge of providing opportunities for these children to demonstrate attainment and give a fair assessment in the context of the primary classroom.

The main categories of talk are:

• group discussion
• telling stories
• describing events
• reading or reciting aloud
• giving instructions.

There are also the listening aspects of these activities. Psychologists and researchers measure language in several ways. They may calculate complexity by counting words and syllables, categorizing grammatical structures or ticking off boxes to check whether the child is arguing, asserting, questioning, responding and so on. These methods may be suitable for intensive study of a small group but are hardly feasible in a busy classroom where the teacher must manage several groups at once. As we saw in the case of Peter and Carl, there is more to communication than words, though the teacher has a framework of language development in mind and knows roughly what children should be doing at each stage. (There is a good staff room reference book on language development for teachers and parents – *Listen to Your Child* by David Crystal.)

Perhaps the most useful area of linguistic theory for the teacher is Pragmatics, or how we use language in a social situation. That social situation could be anything from playing in the playground to doing a group science investigation. We are interested in looking at how children *use* whatever language they have in the classroom situation.

Some points to look for in a practical situation:

- Does the child want to communicate?
- Does the child cope in day-to-day situations despite apparently 'poor' language?
- Can the child use effectively the language he or she has in a learning situation? For example, can he or she join in, talk him or herself through an activity?

At a certain stage a child may find it very difficult to work quietly, needing to verbalize and comment.

The level of the child's language development is a matter for comment on his or her individual profile. If a child is causing concern, and ongoing speech therapy is not available, it may be possible to get a one-off speech therapy assessment which will give a profile and some guidance to the teacher. Although Carl, in the earlier example, had more complex spoken language he showed less willingness to communicate and had few gestures and expressions to aid understanding.

In a further example from a Reception class four children are working together. Andrew and Mark are at a similar level of language development. Charles and Jack are using much more complex language structures. Mark felt out of his depth in the group and the teacher eventually intervened to give Mark a small easy jigsaw to do alongside the others. Andrew wanted to continue working with Charles and Jack. Despite language delay, he sees himself as one of their group, is accepted and works happily. Andrew is determined to stay ahead and wants to be part of the action, using the little language he has to attempt the task in hand. Like Peter he uses one phrase, 'That right', in several ways. He uses it as a question, 'Is it right?', as an assertion, 'It *is* right' and as a statement, 'That's right'. The tone of voice used on the tape leaves one in no doubt as to A's meaning. M gives up at an early stage. The children, all boys, have chosen to do a large jigsaw together. C, who suggested it, has done the jigsaw before and has hidden the picture from the others. They do not know he has done this:

A: That right, that right? (Shows two pieces he has put together)
C: No.
A: That is, that is. It's right M?
M: No. It's not right.

C: That's right, there. One piece done.
A: That right, that right?
J: Don't ask me. That's it. It's wrong. It's wrong.
C: Yeah – hey J, remember when we done that one.
J: Yeah – we've done that by ourselves. (Referring to jigsaw)
C: What if we get another badge?
M: You might not.
C: I hope she says we can. There's a piece.
A: Oh yeah. That right, that right.
C: J, is this right? (Referring to a bit he has done himself)
A: That right?
C: Put them there, the piece that's already made.
A: (Protesting as his wrong bit is rejected) That right! That right!
C: I know, try to fix some of it on to there. Some of it might go on to there.
A: Yeah.
C: It doesn't go there 'cause look, it's hard to get on, it's hard to get on. That's not right.

Andrew wanted to continue working with Charles and Jack and they liked to work with him, despite the differences in language complexity. This illustrates that it is useful to have criteria to record how children use the language they have to function in group and class work.

Language and reading

It has been said that a child can only read what is already in his or her head so language development is important for learning to read, especially if the school uses the 'real book' method, which depends on a certain amount of familiarity with the conventions of fiction and story language. Often teachers will say of a child, 'I don't understand why she can't read when she can talk so well'. It is often the case that reading well is associated with facility in monologue rather than dialogue – with the kind of organization and mental rehearsal that is shown by Lisa in the extract below, rather than Pam's dialogue, which is more *ad hoc* and depends much more on the response partner. Children like Lisa can also describe in sequence what they did in a science experiment or how they made a model. Work on this monologue aspect can be useful, though describing and retelling in pairs may help to begin with.

The following transcripts exemplify what might be expected in the school at each level for retelling a story or describing events. One child in Year 2, asked to describe an event, had it sequenced and organized in her head before she began to relate it:

Adult: What were you telling me about – you were going to do lots of things on Sunday?
L: Five things happened.

Adult: Five things happened – oh, last Sunday, was it? What happened?

L: I had one – the first one was when I was playing with Anna and I fe– we were playing horses and I jumped up and I banged my lip there, and then the one after church. I ban– I was playing on a horse, like that, and I banged my thing there – that's why I've got a bruise.

Adult: What is – oh yes I can see. Yes. What kind of horse is it?

L: A rocking-horse.

Adult: Then what was the next thing?

L: The next thing was when I was playing on the thing again and I fell off the back. No, she was on my back and I tipped up – I either banged my finger on the bannisters or I or I – or I either banged the rocking-horse on the bannisters and so it was hurting and the next one I banged my head on the wall . . .

This example shows that Lisa was used to story language and conventions. She did not assume a shared context to a great extent and she seemed to be trying out the structure 'either . . . or'.

The class teacher advised that the child, Pam, would not say anything and only ever gave one-word answers. Pam had been designated, though not yet statemented, as having special needs. At first she did not respond easily, keeping her head down and muttering, but gradually, as she realized this was meant to be a conversation rather than a question and answer session and she could talk about her home life freely, she began to look up, smile and produce sentences:

Adult: What have you done?

P: It's a drink.

Adult: What is it a drink of?

P: Don't know. (Another child intervenes, 'It's a plant pot')

Adult: Did you really mean it to be a plant pot?

P: No.

Adult: What's your favourite drink?

P: Water.

When we move away from the topic of her work Pam becomes more confident but is obviously wary in case I show disapproval of her family background. When she detects no disapproval she produces more complex language structures, preoccupied by the urge to tell me about her family.

P: My mum is a sister to my aunty . . . and my aunty has got a little boy . . . he went into hospital twice . . . one with his hand broke off and one with his tonsils and his nose done and his ears done . . . When he came down from hospital when he had his tonsils done, right, he went to my house for a long time. He's still at my house now but he's going home now.

Pam had quite a lot to say, in fact, she produced pages of transcript in the end. Her class teacher had 30 other children in the class and had never had time to extend a conversation beyond the one- or two-word answers. Pam needed to gain confidence with a person before she disclosed events in her life. Wells (1986) notes this lack of time to extend and develop a real conversation in the way the child is able to at home. Teachers know too that, although an obvious answer might be to have adult helpers in the classroom to give extra time and attention, care and discretion must be exercised if, for example, another parent were listening to Pam and learning all about her home background.

Some children who have special needs also have difficult or different life circumstances and much of primary classroom talk is about 'ourselves'. If a child feels inhibited about discussing home, for children soon pick up what is acceptable in school, then a whole tranche of language development potential is closed and any difficulties are further compounded.

Planning and providing for children who have special needs in oracy in the primary classroom is not an easy task for the teacher, who must take into account the whole range of attainment. One advantage is that the greatest aid to the development of children's spoken language is interaction with other children – and that resource, at least, is freely available every day.

NOTE

[1] This video is obtainable from the Northern Ireland Curriculum Council, Stranmillis College, Belfast B79 5DY.

REFERENCES

Crystal, D. (1976) *Child Language*. London: Arnolds.
Daniels, H. and Lee, J. (1989) Stories, class and classrooms, *Educational Studies* 15(1) 3–14.
Heath, S. (1983) *Ways with Words*. Cambridge: Cambridge University Press.
Labov, W. (1972) 'The logic of non-standard English'. In Giglioli, P.P. (ed.) *Language and Social Context*. London: Penguin.
Michaels, S. (1981) 'Sharing time: children's narrative styles and differential access to literacy'. In *Language in Society*, vol. 10, pp. 423–43.
Tizard, B. and Hughes, M. (1984) *Young Children Learning*. London: Fontana.
Varkalis, A. (1992) Bilingual and bicultural approaches to art and design, *Journal of Art and Design Education* 11(2), 167–73.
Wells, C.G. (1986) *The Meaning Makers*. London: Heinemann.
Wittgenstein, L. (1961) *Tractatus Logico-Philosophicus*. London: Routledge.

FURTHER READING

Bernstein, B. (1971) *Class, Codes and Control*. London: Routledge.
Des-Fountain, J. (1990) *Using Tape Recorders in Class*. Pamphlet from Waltham Forest Local Education Authority, Essex.
Donaldson, M. (1978) *Children's Minds*. London: Fontana.
Oracy and Special Educational Needs (1992). Occasional papers in oracy, No. 6 NOP, National Curriculum Council.
Wray, D. and Medwell, J. (eds) (1994) *Teaching Primary English*. London: Routledge.

Physical education and dance

Patricia Sanderson

It is unlikely that physical education (PE) would be described as an 'expressive art' and so its inclusion in this book could reasonably be questioned. However, one of the constituents of PE in the National Curriculum is dance which is acknowledged as one of the arts, and dance in turn has many genuine links with gymnastics, games, motor co-ordination and control, but so too is the creative and also the athletics, swimming and outdoor and adventurous activities. An obvious common factor is movement which involves gross as well as fine motor co-ordination and control, but so too is the creative and also the aesthetic dimension, while all aspects of PE offer opportunities for cognitive, personal and social development. PE therefore, can provide a valuable means of all-round education for all children. To benefit from PE, however, a child must have both access to the various activities and the opportunity to take full part in them. In order to do so, some children require special consideration because they have special educational needs (SEN).

Who are the children who have special needs in PE? This question is not as straightforward as it might first appear. The NCC for example points out:

> Some pupils will have a statement of special educational needs (SEN) under the terms of the 1981 *Education Act*, but these pupils may or may not have special needs in physical education. Up to 20% of pupils without a statement have SEN, but again they may or may not have special needs in physical education.
>
> (NCC, 1992, Section E, 1.1)

There are further complications. Some pupils may have SEN *only* in PE, with no real difficulties in any other aspect of the curriculum. Childhood illnesses for example can limit opportunities for motor skill development and control, with extended periods of convalescence being used for extending knowledge and understanding in classroom subjects. A child can quickly get left behind and begin to dread PE lessons. Another consideration is that the subject comprises six activities and it is likely that individual needs will vary accordingly; so too will the level of involvement in each of the processes of planning, performing and evaluating required by the National PE Curriculum. The special needs of the child who is talented must also be taken into account as must those needs which arise from our multicultural society.

Many children in the primary school will therefore have some form of special need in PE but it is usually pupils who have difficulties of a sensory, physical, medical, cognitive or emotional nature who, quite understandably, give rise to feelings of apprehension and some anxiety among teachers. In order to help effectively all the children in a class to benefit from PE a teacher has to understand the nature of any difficulty and learn how to adapt teaching materials, approaches, apparatus and equipment to suit individual needs. To make such efforts a teacher must first be convinced of the value of PE for all children and particularly for those with a special need in one or more physical activity.

THE VALUE OF PHYSICAL EDUCATION

Physical activity plays a crucial role in a child's satisfactory development. The work of Piaget and others have established the relationship between adequate sensori-motor experiences in the early years and later cognitive growth, and it is widely recognized that involvement in a wide range of perceptual-motor and imaginative play activities is of major importance in the sound integrated development of young children. Many teachers and researchers (for example, Jowsey, 1992; Frostig and Maslow, 1973) are so convinced of the importance of physical activity in the development of a wide range of capacities that they argue for increased PE provision, beyond statutory requirements. Those who see the benefits of regular, positive, well-structured PE lessons, maintain that such experiences make valuable contributions to the development of the whole child by offering integrated physical, motor skill, personal and social, cognitive, aesthetic and creative education.

Physical development

The importance of vigorous exercise for the acquisition and maintenance of overall good health is stressed in the National Curriculum document and this reflects general concern at children's sedentary lives and consequent low levels of fitness. Virtually everyone agrees that in today's sophisticated society children do not get enough exercise and this view is consistently confirmed by research at Exeter University (Armstrong, 1990). Indeed it seems that without PE in school some children would get no exercise at all! This certainly appears to be the case with many children with physical or sensory disabilities who often need encouragement to participate fully in PE activities. Over-protection at home and elsewhere has frequently given rise to the erroneous assumption that participation is inadvisable, consequently many of these children are extremely unfit and overweight, while limbs that are mobile are often very weak. Research shows that poor fitness can have serious implications for the development of the heart muscle, possibly causing heart disease in later life (Armstrong, 1990), and this finding alone should be enough to encourage active participation.

McKinley (1980) also points out that strengthening arms and shoulders stabilizes the arm for finer activities such as writing. There are other benefits. Given an adequate diet, children who participate in regular vigorous activity are typically not only fit and strong but also more alert, more aware, stimulated and interested in their surroundings. There is a general feeling of well-being which is also important for effective learning to take place. Children with learning difficulties, for example, especially the subdued and the withdrawn, could benefit considerably from the invigorating effects of regular exercise.

Motor skill co-ordination and development

In the National PE Curriculum, Key Stages (KS) 1 and 2 are recognized as crucially important in the development of basic physical skills, motor control and co-ordination. The rate of development in this area varies greatly and of course those with sensory and physical impairments will have particular difficulties, but levels of attainment could also be limited by restricted environments or other circumstances. Research by Cherrington (1980) for the Leverhulme Foundation for example, showed that the motor development of children raised in high-rise flats was significantly lower than for those raised in other homes. Development can also be limited in homes which are highly disciplined and where play learning activities are undervalued; childhood illness has already been referred to as a possible cause of poor motor co-ordination and of course predominantly sedentary lifestyles give few opportunities for the extended practice which is fundamental to skill acquisition.

Whatever the cause, clumsiness can be a source of great distress to a child and it is of crucial importance that opportunities are taken in PE to improve skill levels. If, throughout the primary school, a child shows a lack of body awareness (indicated by, for example, regularly bumping into others, knocking over equipment, or tripping up), poor hand-eye co-ordination (for example, difficulty in throwing, catching and hitting) and difficulty in keeping to a simple skipping rhythm then the opportunities to join in recreational play activities will become increasingly limited. Gordon and McKinley (1980) describe how such children come to dread PE and point to a number of studies linking clumsiness with emotional and behavioural problems. The erosion of self-confidence and self-esteem can be severe. Knight (1993), for instance, refers to research which shows that long-term lack of physical competency can affect academic achievement. PE therefore presents a vitally important opportunity to make a positive impact on a SEN which can have widespread repercussions. An indication of the extent of the problem is that between 5 and 10 per cent of pupils in mainstream schools apparently have some form of motor difficulty with boys sometimes outnumbering girls in a ratio of 2:1.

The needs of the talented child should also be borne in mind and these are also recognized by the National PE Curriculum document. Children who are gifted in the area of motor skill should be given the same opportunities to develop their special talent as those with outstanding abilities in other areas. Otherwise frustration can lead to emotional and behavioural problems.

Cognitive development

The relationship between perceptual motor experience and cognitive development has been the focus of a considerable amount of research, particularly in the USA. Kephart (1960), for example, in his influential book *The Slow Learner in the Classroom* stresses the importance of additional movement experiences for those children whose limited environments and lifestyles have failed to provide them with the sensori-motor experiences necessary to establish the 'readiness' or basic skills which are prerequisites for the development of the complex activities of reading, writing and arithmetic. For instance, before eye-hand co-ordination can develop a child must first be able to distinguish right and left sides of the body and control two sides separately and simultaneously. These factors are also related to reading readiness.

In more general terms the psychologist Cratty (1974) has pointed out that PE and dance lessons are likely to have the greatest impact on overall intellectual functioning if the child is actively involved in decision-making and devising solutions to problems. The strong motivating effect on classroom learning of success in movement classes, improvement in self-image and in social relationships, and the feeling of well-being and alertness resulting from participation in physical activities should also be borne in mind.

Physical education and dance experiences can also be very helpful for those children who have difficulty in forming concepts because of problems in integrating information from different senses. For instance, exploration in movement of spatial concepts such as bigger and smaller, higher and lower, forwards, backwards and sideways has been found to promote understanding of the appropriate verbal and written symbols. The additional information supplied by the kinaesthetic receptors in muscles and joints can be particularly valuable too, for children with sensory impairments.

Personal and social development

By helping to promote co-ordination, strength, fitness, skill and understanding in PE lessons, the teacher can play a fundamental part in a child's social development, as these attributes are important in enabling a child to join with others in recreational activities. Many children who are rejected at play can become withdrawn, defensive and aggressive.

Through PE lessons, teachers can also help children learn how to play with others, to co-operate, to share equipment and ideas, take turns and learn to accept defeat, while being encouraged to persevere to attain success. These are important for all children but more so for those whose disability has often meant isolation and little inter-action. Kitson (1993) points out that PE experiences are helpful for those who avoid social contact such as autistic children. Riley (1993) also refers to the role of PE in reducing the social isolation of many children with learning difficulties who for various reasons avoid contact with others. Although the National Curriculum stresses the competitive aspect of PE, the essential co-operative component of the activities should be constantly underlined. Besides, children enjoy helping each other when such an atmosphere is encouraged. Morgan and Saunders (1993), for example, report that children in their school were very sympathetic, sensitive and willing to adapt material when working with those with physical impairments. No one ever avoided working with them. There will however be occasions when children have to be encouraged to be patient and adaptable and this is an important part of their own personal development.

Acceptance by others is a necessary part of satisfactory emotional development. The degree of success in school is also a factor and PE can play an important part here too, for it is possible for all children to achieve some success and merit genuine praise.

There are other contributions. For physically disabled children, developing a positive self-image is related to correcting an overly negative view of their abilities while coming to terms with what they can and cannot do. Autistic children and those with sight impairments have limited body awareness, and so involvement in PE activities can be particularly useful in helping to develop body concept and consequently self-image. The concept of the body in relation to space that is above, behind, near and far, can also be developed in order to reduce the vulnerability and disorientation experienced by these children.

Aesthetic development

Dance, as an expressive art form, is readily acknowledged as contributing to aesthetic education but surprise is often expressed when it is suggested that other PE activities can also contribute in this way. Most children find movement itself intrinsically pleasurable; many teachers, for instance, report that movement lessons are the first occasions when some children smile. It could be argued that the aesthetic is a prime motivator for taking part and also persevering in PE, for it relates to enjoyment. It is important therefore that *all* children should be helped to experience the pleasurable sensations and feelings which arise from running, jumping, rolling, climbing, swimming, moving rhythmically to music, throwing, catching, hitting a ball, and so on. Many children from deprived environments or with restricted lifestyles have limited knowledge of the tactile pleasures of moving through water for instance. The possibilities for immediate aesthetic pleasures in PE and dance are vast and open to all children regardless of ability or background. The simplest movement can provide sensations and feelings which give great enjoyment to a child and as skill and sensitivity develop, the teacher can present further opportunities for more refined and extensive aesthetic experiences. The delight in the initial acquisition of a skill, such as catching a ball, moving in harmony with a musical rhythm, becoming waterborne, and completing a forward roll can be recreated in the persistent repetition which fascinates young children. Subsequently satisfaction is gained in constructing sequences in gymnastics and dance, inventing a new game and being part of a team or group when co-operation produces a good performance. For some children such feelings of aesthetic pleasure are rare and the opportunities to experience them in PE and dance should not be easily dismissed nor the value of such a source of aesthetic knowledge and experience underestimated.

Aesthetic sensibilities awakened by means of movement experiences can be enhanced by encouraging children to become more alert to visual aesthetic qualities in physical activities. The National PE Curriculum requires that children are taught to evaluate their own and other's performances in a variety of contexts and these are in effect aesthetic evaluations, for the focus is on the *quality*, completing a movement however simple, as well as possible. Watching each other perform well-executed gymnastics or dance sequences, observing a game well played, appreciating the performance of a dance company in a theatre or at school, can all promote aesthetic awareness and interest. Participating in and watching PE activities can make children more conscious of qualities such as beauty, grace, power, shape and help them acquire basic aesthetic concepts of form and expression. The aesthetic is an important dimension of PE which is accessible to all. It also provides a valuable modification to competition which can exclude so many children when carried to excess.

Creative development

Growth in aesthetic understanding is closely associated with creative development in PE and dance. Children discover how different parts of the body move in relation to each other and how contrasting rhythms, dynamics, patterns and pathways can be combined to give very different results. Encounters with a wide range of equipment and apparatus stimulate the learning of new skills, extending the potential for additional creative experiences. Opportunities to devise games, gymnastic sequences and dances give insights into the creative process which involves experimentation, selection and rejection before movements can be combined into a satisfying whole.

Such creative experiences are open to all children. A physically disabled child, notwithstanding a limited movement range, can produce very original well-structured movement phrases and devise interesting, demanding games sometimes involving other children, sometimes alone. It is also often the case that children who have difficulties with verbal or written language symbols thrive when given the opportunity to be inventive in the medium of movement. These children often surprise their teachers with the individuality of their responses and the complexity of the forms they construct. Dance is particularly valuable for those children who are frustrated by a limited facility with the spoken or written word (frustration which can lead to behaviour disturbance) enabling them to express and communicate feelings and ideas through an alternative medium.

Participation in dances or games which are already established, that is devised by others including the teacher, have a part to play in developing understanding of the creative process, for it is important that children experience a complete structure, an end-product. Physical involvement in a whole game, dance or gymnastic sequence, helps a child understand how parts fit together to form a whole thus acquiring crucial knowledge relating to the key concepts of structure and form, and clarifying what is meant by 'a game', 'a dance', 'a phrase', 'a sequence' and so on. Information obtained by the child in the role of spectator makes similar contributions to creative development. Such concrete experiences are an important part of learning in the creative domain for all children but particularly for those who have difficulty in making connections and seeing relationships.

Creative interpretation however, whether as performer or observer does not appear to be directly related to intellectual skills and can often compensate for limited physical abilities too. We are all aware of the child whose inventive approach to a game gives an advantage over someone more technically skilful or intellectually gifted; or the dancer whose expressive qualities overcome other limitations. These are important aspects of creative understanding which should be borne in mind by the teacher of children with special educational needs in PE.

THE AIM OF PHYSICAL EDUCATION

The overall aim of PE in the primary school is the integrated physical, motor skill, cognitive, personal and social, aesthetic and creative development of each child, including anyone with SEN.

Each of the physical activities – dance, gymnastics, games, swimming, athletics, outdoor and adventurous activities – which together comprise the National PE Curriculum, can make distinctive as well as general contributions to this overall aim. For example:

1. Dance:
   - is easily accessible to children with a wide range of special needs as no equipment or apparatus is involved
   - emphasizes individual interpretation, so that everyone can gain immediate success whatever the nature of any movement limitations, with a consequent boost to self-confidence and esteem
   - offers extensive possibilities for aesthetic and creative growth by means of the expression and communication of feelings and ideas, through a structured movement form
   - an alternative means of communication which is particularly welcome for those frustrated by a limited facility with the spoken or written word, frustration which can lead to behaviour disturbance
   - for those children with behaviour difficulties, offers opportunities for the safe release of tensions, for aggressive feelings and emotions to be expressed physically, but within an artistic form
   - enables fitness, co-ordination, balance, rhythmic skills and mobility all to be developed
   - enables basic spatial awareness and associated vocabulary to be improved

- enables a positive body concept and self-image to be promoted
- helps understanding of other cultures.

2. Gymnastic activity:
   - develops controlled management of the body
   - can improve flexibility, strength, endurance, co-ordination, balance and mobility
   - involves children in the creative process
   - helps promote aesthetic growth by focusing on *how* a movement is performed
   - may contribute to cognitive growth through specific perceptual motor experiences
   - improves spatial awareness and body concept.

3. Games experiences:
   - offer the possibility of developing fitness and cardiovascular health
   - help improve motor control in the basic skills of walking, running and jumping
   - develop more complex motor skills involving eye-hand and eye-foot co-ordination
   - give *all* children knowledge of an important aspect of our culture, which can also help social integration
   - contribute to creative growth and understanding
   - help promote cognitive growth
   - develop an appreciation of the aesthetic aspects of sport.

4. Swimming:
   - is an activity which can be enjoyed throughout life regardless of physical or cognitive ability
   - provides excellent all-round exercise
   - proficiency is necessary in order to take part in other water sports such as sailing, water-skiing, surfing and canoeing
   - skills are essential in an island replete with rivers, canals and lakes, for survival
   - provides an important source of aesthetic experience
   - releases tensions and promotes a feeling of well-being.

5. Athletic activities contribute to the development of:
   - the fundamental skills of running, jumping, throwing and catching
   - flexibility
   - suppleness
   - muscular strength
   - endurance
   - cardiovascular health.

6. Outdoor and adventurous activities:
   - develop stamina, endurance and perseverance
   - promote safe responses to contrasting situations

- develop a respect for the environment
- promote an aesthetic appreciation of urban and rural environments
- improves motor co-ordination
- promote creative responses to challenges.

THE NATIONAL PHYSICAL EDUCATION CURRICULUM

The revised National Curriculum for physical education (DFE, 1995) emphasizes that PE should be accessible to all children. Consequently Programmes of Study (PoS) for KS1 and KS2 contain elements which can be taught to pupils in ways appropriate to their abilities. Provision is also made for the small number at either end of the ability range to work from earlier or later KS PoS. Thus greater flexibility has been introduced so that the need for modifications and disapplications of the PE curriculum is reduced, although this will not remove the need for the teacher to continue to adopt imaginative approaches in order to integrate a child with a special need into an activity. The additional knowledge and skills needed will be discussed in the final section of this chapter.

The main points of the National PE Curriculum are:

- There is no separate Attainment Target. The latter simply comprises the End of Key Stage Descriptions.
- Physical education should involve pupils in the continuous process of planning, performing and evaluating. Although the greatest emphasis should be placed on the actual performance, the inclusion of planning and evaluating offers opportunities to fully involve every child, for some measure of genuine success can be achieved in one or more of these areas. For instance the clumsy child or one confined to a wheelchair, could gain status with peers because of the good ideas suggested for a game or a dance, the evaluation of a gymnastic sequence could reveal acute perceptual skills, while a child with learning difficulties could very well shine when it comes to the performance of a skill. PE also offers opportunities to the teacher to fulfil the Common Requirement to help pupils express themselves clearly in speech; it may be a particularly appropriate context in which to encourage and give confidence to those with language difficulties.
- There are three parts to the Programmes of Study:
  1. Common Requirements. These are largely concerned with ensuring access to the whole of the PE curriculum for the great majority of pupils, whatever their particular SEN might be.
  2. General Requirements for physical education which are applic-

able across all Key Stages. There are three points relating to the promotion of: physical activity and healthy lifestyles, positive attitudes and safe practice.

3. Separate activity specific PoS for each of the Key Stages.

- At KS1 the activity specific PoS is divided into three sections relating to games, gymnastics and dance. Throughout the Key Stage pupils should be taught about the changes that occur to their bodies as they exercise and also to recognize the short-term effects of exercise on the body.

- The activity specific PoS at KS2 comprises six sections with swimming, athletics, outdoor and adventurous activities additional to games, gymnastics and dance. Schools however may choose to teach swimming at KS1. Throughout the Key Stage pupils should be taught how to sustain energetic activity over appropriate periods of time in a range of physical activities as well as the short-term effects of exercise on the body. The statutory requirement to teach such a wide range of activities means that every child should be able to develop proficiency in at least one area, which is vitally important for a healthy lifestyle, self-esteem and social integration.

- There are End of Key Stage Descriptions (EKSDs) for KS1 and for KS2. These have been designed to help teachers judge their pupils' attainment in relation to these expectations, in terms of planning, performing and evaluating across all aspects of PE. It is likely that individual achievement will vary in each of these areas according to the activity.

Common Requirements

Appropriate provision must be made for pupils who need to use:

> means of communication other than speech, including computers, technological aids, signing, symbols or lip reading ... methods of acquiring information in a non-visual or non-aural way ... technological aids in producing written work ... aids to allow access to practical activities within and beyond school.
>
> (DFE, 1995, p. 113)

This kind of provision is required in order to ensure access to the whole of the National Curriculum for all children, but there are specific implications for PE. Additional teaching assistance may be necessary if there is a child with physical, sensory or behavioural difficulties in the class. It is likely too that additional equipment will be required and existing apparatus adapted depending upon the special need. For example, a wider range of flotation aids in swimming; bats and balls which are lighter, larger and generally more easily handled and controlled; thicker mats for gymnastics; equipment of contrasting shapes, textures and colours; additional percussive instruments for dance. The Common Requirements also state that, where necessary, PE activities must be adapted, so that no child is excluded.

In order to ensure this, and also help all children progress and demonstrate achievement in PE, teachers need to develop their own knowledge and understanding of the subject. Appropriate INSET and the support of the school's PE curriculum co-ordinator will help the teacher do this. There will be further discussion of these important issues in the final section of this chapter.

General Requirements

In addition to involving pupils in the continuous process of planning, performing and evaluating – although greatest emphasis should be placed on actual performance – the following requirements apply to the teaching of PE across all Key Stages.

The promotion of physical activity and healthy lifestyles. To achieve this, children should be taught throughout their school life the importance of:

> being physically active ... having good posture and generally using the body correctly ... involvement in activities that develop cardio-vascular health, flexibility, muscular strength and endurance ... personal hygiene in relation to vigorous activity.
>
> (DFE, 1995, p. 114)

All of these factors are applicable to all pupils although both the teacher and any child concerned, will have to be aware of medical conditions such as asthma, heart problems and cystic fibrosis which necessarily limit the degree of physical exertion. But exercise *is* important and in these and other cases positively helpful, so that a disability should not be used as an excuse for avoiding PE. Understanding the importance of physical activity and personal hygiene can also be promoted in the classroom. Such knowledge could prove to be a motivating factor for those pupils whose impairments mean that many aspects of PE constantly present challenges to them.

The development of positive attitudes. To promote this ideal pupils should be taught:

> to observe the conventions of fair play, honest competition and good sporting behaviour as team members, individual participants and

spectators . . . how to deal with success and limitations in performance . . . to try hard to consolidate their performances . . . to be
aware of others and the environment.

(ibid.)

These behaviours are applicable particularly to those children who
have no special needs in PE themselves but who are in a class with
those who have. They need to learn how to be considerate towards
others, to be tolerant of those with limited expertise and that
winning, although important, is not all-important. The child who
has special abilities in any aspect of PE is especially vulnerable to the
problems of success and failure which can have widespread
repercussions. On the other hand, those with physical, sensory or
motor difficulties have often been cosseted at home with the result
that they can begin to expect to get their own way in many
situations, including PE. For similar reasons many do not feel the
need to work hard to improve a performance.

Safe practice. To ensure this, children should be taught:

to respond readily to instructions . . . to recognise and follow relevant
rules, laws, codes, etiquette and safety procedures for different
activities or events in practice and during competition . . . why
particular clothing, footwear and protection are worn for different
activities . . . the risks to safety of wearing inappropriate clothing,
footwear and jewellery . . . how to lift, carry, place and use equipment
safely . . . to warm up for and recover from exercise.

(ibid.)

Safe practice is of fundamental importance in PE lessons for all
children, more so when there are those with special needs in the
class, and so this aspect of teaching PE will be returned to in the next
section of this chapter. The strict adherence to instructions and rules
is particularly relevant to those with sensory and also emotional
problems, for they need the security of precise limits and procedures.
Lack of knowledge concerning the correct handling apparatus can be
dangerous, causing injury as well as exacerbating existing physical
difficulties. Appropriate clothing for those with physical disabilities
is also relevant as these children can easily become cold, while the
clothing and jewellery traditions of some ethnic and religious groups
require consideration. Awareness is vital from an early age, of the
importance of adequate warm-up for and a recovery from exercise to
avoid injury, again particularly for those with physical impairments.

Subject specific Programmes of Study: Key Stages 1 and 2

During KS1 pupils should be encouraged to develop simple skills, to learn to link actions together, to practise, to begin to work with a partner, to talk about and make simple judgements about their own and others' performances, to recognize and describe the changes that happen to their bodies during exercise.

During KS2 pupils should be able to practise, improve, refine and repeat movements with increasing control and accuracy; find solutions to challenges, sometimes imaginatively; work successfully alone, with others and as members of a team; make judgements on their own and others' performances and use this information to improve their own work; sustain energetic activity over periods of time and show they understand what is happening to their bodies during exercise.

It is evident that children with SEN in PE, whether these are due to physical, sensory, motor, emotional, medical or other difficulties, are going to need specific help from the teacher in order to show these kinds of behaviours in each PE activity, and this will be dealt with later in this chapter. Meanwhile it is worth looking at the National Curriculum for each area of activity at both Key Stages, noting those aspects where special provision is likely to be necessary so that all children can be fully integrated into the class.

Games

At **KS1** pupils should be taught:

- simple competitive games, including how to play them as individuals and, when ready, in pairs and small groups;
- to develop and practise a variety of ways of sending (including throwing, striking, rolling and bouncing), receiving and travelling with a ball or other similar games equipment;
- elements of games play that include running, chasing, dodging, awareness of space and other players.

(DFE, 1995, p. 115)

At **KS2** pupils should be taught:

- to understand and play small sided games and simplified versions of recognized competitive team and individual games, covering the following types – invasion, *e.g. mini-soccer, netball*, striking/ fielding, *e.g. rounders, small-sided cricket*, net/wall, *e.g. short tennis*;
- to explore and understand common skills and principles, including attack and defence in invasion, striking/fielding, net/wall and target games;
- to improve the skills of sending, receiving, striking and travelling with a ball in the above games.

(ibid.)

Games can present difficulties to many children because they are such complex activities. The apparently straightforward task of throwing and catching a ball demands sophisticated hand-eye co-ordination. When a hand-held implement is introduced the difficulties are multiplied. Extensive practice and perseverance is therefore needed in order to acquire the various basic skills and then link them together, more so for the child with motor problems.

It is crucial that work on skill development begins at an early age, otherwise it will be increasingly difficult for some children to be fully involved in any kind of game where there are other participants and rules to take into account. Skills need to be broken down into stages as necessary, ensuring that success is achieved and frustration minimized. Those with sensory impairments need the aspects of a task enhancing, such as strengthening auditory cues or enlarging visual aspects. There may also have to be some adaptation of equipment and modification of games played. These considerations also apply to those with physical difficulties and particularly as far as invasion-type games are concerned. Children with learning difficulties may be very good at acquiring particular skills, but may need help in working with a partner or as a member of a team and in comprehending what is meant by co-operation, fair competition and, in the case of upper juniors, tactics.

Gymnastic activities

At **KS1** pupils should be taught:

- different ways of performing the basic actions of travelling using hands and feet, turning, rolling, jumping, balancing, swinging, climbing, both on the floor and using apparatus;
- to link a series of actions both on the floor and using apparatus, and how to repeat them.

(DFE, 1995, p 115)

At **KS2** pupils should be taught:

- different means of rolling, jumping, swinging, balancing and travelling on hands and feet, and how to adapt, practise and refine these actions, both on the floor and using apparatus;
- practise, refine and repeat a longer series of actions, making increasingly complex movement sequences both on the floor and using apparatus;
- to emphasise changes of shape, speed and direction through gymnastic actions.

(ibid.)

Gymnastics lessons present fewer problems than games in that each child in a class can be fully involved working individually according to his or her capabilities. Apparatus can be adapted and arranged so that everyone, including those with mobility problems can succeed and make progress. Children with learning difficulties are likely to need help in linking actions together and in remembering sequences. Children with emotional problems will also need assistance as they do not find it easy to concentrate. As gymnastic activity is particularly valuable in developing motor co-ordination and control, children should be encouraged to repeat and practise basic actions. Those whose body management is limited, need to be given the time to explore and experiment in order to gather the fundamental movement skills needed to make further progress. By breaking down a gymnastic skill into its component parts, achievable intermediate goals are provided for the child as is, in this way, the success which is so important.

Dance

At **KS1** pupils should be taught:

- to develop control, co-ordination, balance, poise and elevation in basic actions of travelling, jumping, turning, gesture and stillness;
- to explore movements or patterns, including some from existing dance traditions;
- to explore moods and feelings and to develop their response to music through dances, by using rhythmic responses and contrasts of speed, shape, direction and level.

(DFE, 1995, p. 115)

At **KS2** pupils should be taught:

- to compose and control their movements by varying shape, size, direction, level, speed, tension and continuity;
- a number of dance forms from different times and places, including some traditional dances of the British Isles;
- to express feelings, moods and ideas, to respond to music and to create simple characters and narratives in movement in response to a range of stimuli through dance.

(ibid.)

Dance, unlike the other aspects of PE, is concerned fundamentally with expression and communication. Movement is therefore used as a means to this end, it is non-competitive and, as no equipment or apparatus is involved, all children can take part safely. Nevertheless when a wheelchair or mobility aid is necessary, everyone in the class must learn to be continually alert so that no collisions occur. This also applies when those with sensory impairments are involved. Children with motor problems are likely to need some help with specific rhythms, such as skipping or those of dances from other times and places, children with learning difficulties may need the teacher's assistance in devising dances, remembering and repeating them, and also describing what others have done. The requirement to use a wide range of stimuli is an advantage in capturing and maintaining the interest of those whose concentration is poor, while percussion is particularly useful for those with hearing difficulties. The use of videotapes of dance performances, theatre visits and possibly the residency of a 'dance in education' company are all invaluable teaching aids, which are relevant to all children whatever their needs, and which will help the teacher fulfil the National Curriculum requirements.

Swimming

Swimming may be taught in either **KS1** or **KS2**. During either or both of these periods, pupils should be taught:

- to develop confidence in water, and how to rest, float and adopt support positions;
- a variety of means of propulsion using either arms or legs or both, and develop effective and efficient swimming strokes on front and back:
- to swim unaided, competently and safely, for at least 25 metres;
- the principles and skills of water safety and survival.

(DFE, 1995, p. 117)

Swimming is a physical activity which can be enjoyed by virtually everyone regardless of physical or cognitive ability. In order to take charge of a class however, a teacher must have a Royal Life Saving Society (RLSS) life saving qualification, although most LEAs have their own qualified instructors, leaving the teacher free to give individual attention to any child with special needs. Additional specialized help will be needed for anyone with a physical disability, not only for safe entry and exit from the water, but also to ensure that there is no possibility of injury as a result of mishandling during the lesson. Help will also be needed if there is anyone with behaviour problems in the class, for safety reasons. Medical conditions must also be taken into account and any instructor informed accordingly. For example, pupils with ear ailments should be excluded from jumping, diving and underwater swimming and partially sighted children need the permission of a consultant ophthalmologist. Swimming aids must also be available, appropriate to individual needs.

Athletic activities

Pupils should be taught:

- to develop and practise basic techniques in running, *e.g., over short distances, over long distances, in relays,* throwing, *e.g., for accuracy/ distance*, and jumping, *e.g., for height/distance*, using a variety of equipment;

- to measure, compare and improve their own performance.

(ibid.)

In order to make all athletic activities accessible in some way to children with physical difficulties, tasks must be adapted for those using wheelchairs and ambulant aids, while in any relay event, it is good teaching practice to ensure a mixture of abilities within individual teams, including those with motor problems. Children without any SEN in PE need to learn how to adapt to those who have. Measures – particularly in relation to safety – will have to be taken to ensure the full involvement of those with sensory difficulties. The improvement of personal performance also needs to be stressed, rather than the competition between individuals. Children with learning difficulties are likely to need help with measuring and comparing.

Outdoor and adventurous activities

Pupils should be taught:

- to perform outdoor and adventurous activities, *e.g. orienteering exercises*, in one or more different environment(s), *e.g. playground, school grounds, parks, woodland, seashore*;
- challenges of a problem-solving nature, *e.g. negotiating obstacle courses*, using suitable equipment, e.g. gymnastic or adventure play apparatus, whilst working individually and with others;
- the skills necessary for the activities undertaken.

(ibid.)

The degree of additional help needed in order to involve all the children in the class will depend upon the environment chosen by, or made available to the teacher. For example, a greater level of planning, organization and supervision will be needed in the countryside than in the school grounds, although in adventure parks there should be arrangements in place to accommodate those with most kinds of special needs.

To a large extent the accessibility or otherwise of the National PE Curriculum to all children is dependent upon good teaching practice. Well-structured lessons with clear objectives and good organization are essential. If, for example, the rhythm of the lesson is constantly interrupted because of insufficient equipment, then the attention and interest of some children will be lost irretrievably. Similarly, rules and routines for bringing out and replacing apparatus should be strictly adhered to for the benefit of all children and particularly those who have sensory impairments or behaviour difficulties. Nevertheless specific information on the limitations imposed by certain medical and other conditions on participation in PE is essential, and in the first instance guidance should be sought from parents and medical advisers. A publication by The British Association of Advisers and Lecturers in Physical Education (1989) is also useful in this regard in listing the various conditions and the associated limitations as far as PE is concerned, while the Further Reading section of this chapter and Useful Addresses at the end of this book provide details of various curriculum materials and organizations which can give additional information the teacher needs. The next part of this chapter is also devoted to the consideration of the main issues involved in teaching children with a wide range of needs and abilities in PE.

TEACHING CHILDREN WITH A RANGE OF NEEDS AND ABILITIES

Physical education can make valuable contributions to the physical, motor skill, personal and social, cognitive, aesthetic and creative development of *all* children. However, if each child in a class which includes a wide spectrum of abilities and backgrounds is to gain the greatest possible benefit from experiences in games, gymnastics, dance, swimming, athletics, outdoor and adventurous activities, then lessons must be well structured with clear objectives and sound organization, taking into account the various individual needs of pupils. Teachers must be both positive and imaginative in their approaches, willing to reconsider established practices, methods and materials for instance, in order to maximize the learning capacity of every child. Special consideration must be given to the provision of safe, secure teaching and learning environments so that the child can participate fully with others and be totally integrated into the class. For clarity of presentation this section is subdivided into teaching approaches, the teacher–child relationship, safety, class management and special needs in PE, although there is obviously considerable overlap across these areas.

Teaching approaches

In order to help children learn, a teacher must be imaginative and flexible in the approaches adopted, the more so if there are those with special educational needs in a class. Teacher intervention can be both direct and indirect and, although the stress in PE and dance in primary schools is on the latter, there is room for both approaches, emphases varying both within and between lessons according to the needs of individuals and the immediate objectives of the teacher.

For the most part the teacher is in the role of initiator and guide, taking as a starting point what a child can do rather than focus on a specific end-product. Children respond individually within the limitations set by the teacher and in this way a child can grow in confidence and independence. Personal interpretation is valued and skill develops gradually along with awareness of qualitative aspects of movement and inventiveness. This informal situation whereby children are given opportunities to think for themselves, to explore and experiment can greatly benefit those who are inhibited by tension and anxiety (often due to memories of frequent failure) if asked to conform to a precise way of moving. With this approach progress is individual and so all children can experience success. In order to stimulate children to improve their movement responses and therefore to become more skilful and to help them create novel, well-structured sequences, games or dances, a teacher calls upon a variety of techniques including demonstrations, questions, suggestions and comments. A child with a specific educational need may respond more positively to one particular technique rather than another, and therefore a teacher needs to be aware of not only the potential of each one for learning when used separately and in combination but also the needs of the individual.

Demonstrations by the teacher, by children or by means of videotape recordings are powerful means of communicating information and capturing interest and attention. In particular, children with learning difficulties can benefit more readily from moving visual images than from verbal explanations. If children are being asked to notice aspects of a performance then the demonstration must be of a limited length and of good quality for the same reasons that blackboard work should always be of a high standard. Reasons for asking a child to demonstrate could be to motivate, raise morale or integrate more into the class. Obviously any demonstration must be relevant and a good illustration of a particular point, otherwise the child could be open to ridicule with serious consequences for personal development. It needs to be stressed however that a valuable demonstration should not be interpreted as spectacular movement. The originality of the work or the careful execution could well be aspects to which attention is being drawn.

Questions are important means of focusing a child's attention and helping concentration, thereby avoiding the onset of the aimless behaviour which often precedes disruptive incidents. Questions can greatly assist learning when they are associated with a demonstration or when a child is working independently, for they can present a challenge to greater effort, inventiveness and clarification. A teacher's suggestions also have a place in encouraging creative work by initiating exploration or stimulating the imagination, thereby engendering confidence among some children. On the other hand, care must be taken to avoid suppressing independence in the insecure child or one whose lack of confidence causes reluctance to offer personal ideas when those of the teacher automatically appear to be far superior.

Underpinning all teaching, of course, should be the regular praise ✓ and encouragement which most children need but especially those for whom progress is slow. Whenever possible comments should be positive although favourable remarks should always be followed by a challenging question or suggestion, the aim constantly being to improve a response and expand awareness.

The broad analysis of movement usually attributed to Rudolf Laban is a useful aid to the teacher. This analysis draws attention to the major constituents of movement namely the body moving in space with varying dynamics, in relation to other people, apparatus or equipment. Thus when observing a child a teacher might consider:

- *what* the body is doing and which parts are being used
- *where* the movement is going in the space
- *how* the movement is accomplished, that is, the dynamic quality
- *with whom or what* the movement is accomplished.

Using this summary a teacher can more readily help a child by analysing the movements and seeing more precisely where assistance is needed, whether this is in the accurate performance of a skill or a more imaginative interpretation of a task.

This analysis and the techniques referred to can also be usefully employed when a direct, precise method of teaching is required as, for example, when safety factors are involved. Children must be shown the correct way to lift and carry apparatus, and learn to land and roll safely so that injury is avoided. Direct intervention by the teacher is also sometimes necessary for the acquisition of other fundamental skills such as taking the weight on the hands or travelling to a specific rhythm. Occasionally it is appropriate to manipulate a child through a movement physically, a swimming stroke for example, as this may be the only means whereby the child can gain relevant kinaesthetic information and experience the feelings associated with completing a movement correctly. If a physically disabled child is involved, a teacher must, of course, be scrupulously familiar with the child's limitations and potential capabilities.

Direct teaching may involve the whole class although here the maturity of the children is a factor. Juniors respond positively to fairly extensive periods of formal teaching, whereas with infants whose concentration is much shorter this kind of intervention must necessarily be brief and interspersed with periods of exploration and experimentation. For the most part, a direct approach will be used when dealing with individuals. Children with learning difficulties, for example, benefit considerably as the teacher can ensure that incidental information which such children often fail to pick up, is recognized and absorbed. Emotionally disturbed children also enjoy the security of this approach.

Working towards a narrow, clearly specified goal can also give a sense of purpose to many children and when success is achieved it can be readily acknowledged as it conforms to a recognizable model. The positive effects in terms of motivation and self-image are enormous and of great importance to children for whom success is not a regular occurrence in other areas of the curriculum. On the other hand, the possibility of failure is ever present, with its dire consequences. The teacher must therefore ensure that the child does succeed either by modifying the objectives or breaking down the skill and setting intermediate, achievable goals.

A judicious combination of direct and indirect methods of teaching PE and dance activities is most likely to help a child's physical, motor skill, personal and social, cognitive, aesthetic and creative development.

The teacher–child relationship

Most teachers recognize that a good relationship with a child is necessary for effective learning to take place. When the vulnerable child is involved, however, one who has met with persistent failure or who is withdrawn, disturbed or has other difficulties, it is absolutely vital that the child likes and trusts the teacher. Confidence can be at a very low ebb and it is the teacher's task to restore self-respect; PE situations where the overall environment is very different from that of the classroom can present ideal opportunities for a teacher to form a good relationship with a child. An observant teacher can also become aware of a difficulty during PE lessons which has not come to light elsewhere; evidence of a potential physical or sensory impairment for instance, a problem with co-ordination, poor spatial awareness, inability to form sequences. Difficulties with undressing and dressing for PE are early and clear indications of clumsiness. Sometimes a teacher by merely recognizing and accepting a difficulty can greatly reduce a child's anxieties.

The relationship between a teacher and a child with special needs should perhaps be more accurately described as a partnership, with the teacher guiding the child through the learning process when necessary to ensure that success is experienced. A child can feel isolated if he or she is the only child in the class with a particular impairment and the teacher needs to work hard to ensure integration. Sometimes it is the acclaim of peers which a child requires to boost confidence and here a teacher can structure situations so that the necessary approval is received. All children with special needs crave praise and encouragement much more frequently than most other children; advantages of PE and dance situations include the numerous opportunities which occur regularly when praise can be given and also recognized as genuine by the child concerned, which is of course a most important factor.

The teacher's own enthusiasm and positive attitude can be a key factor in developing not only confidence but also continuing interest in PE and dance. Active involvement, being a child's partner in a game for instance or joining in a group sequence can help cement all-important contacts between teacher and child. A warm and caring relationship with a child really is the key to satisfactory progress, thereby optimizing the opportunities available in PE and dance for fitness, recreation, aesthetic and creative enjoyment.

Safe practice

The fundamental importance of safe practice in PE and dance is stressed in the National PE Curriculum and this General Requirement is underlined further when there are children with special needs in the class. The special conditions pertaining to swimming have been referred to previously and good class management, obviously a major constituent of a safe environment, will be considered more fully later in this section.

Teachers are often unduly fearful when working with children who have physical or sensory disabilities, yet if sensible precautions are taken there is no reason why they should not be fully integrated into the class. Lack of adequate information is the usual cause of excessive caution. A teacher needs to know exactly what limitations there are on physical involvement, the range and extent of the impairment, any medication prescribed and information on any particular ways of handling. No child should be put at risk but on the other hand a child with a physical or sensory difficulty should be encouraged to lead as active a life as possible.

Full background information gives the teacher the confidence necessary to develop a child's independence and initiative, and to discourage over-protectiveness in others. Texts such as BAALPE (1989) and Jowsey (1992) are well worth consulting as they provide very useful guidance and reassurance.

As far as the indoor physical environment is concerned, an important consideration for those who are clumsy or who have an impairment is that the floor should be unpolished to reduce the possibility of slipping. Playgrounds should be smooth enough for a wheelchair or walking aid to be used without difficulty, although the child concerned must also be aware of natural hazards such as grids, sinks and so on; stones in grass can be another problem. When using a wheelchair or walking aid a child should be free to explore the space and not be confined to one area for 'safety'; other children in the class therefore need to be aware of their own responsibility in allowing the extra space and time a disabled child needs but without isolation. Similarly, children with limited sight and hearing often have poor spatial awareness and are therefore more likely to collide with others, so in this case too other children need to adapt their behaviour. Sensory impairments also demand the combined use of visual and aural stopping signals by the teacher and, as far as possible, consistency in the placement and organization of apparatus, membership of apparatus groups and so on to avoid confusion. There are a number of opportunities during gymnastics and dance lessons when a wheelchair or walking aid could be discarded with advantage to the child. Extra mats are likely to be needed and care should be taken that a child does not become over-tired, although periodic rather than constant involvement in a lesson should overcome that problem.

Those with physical difficulties should be adequately clothed during PE lessons both indoors and outside. Movements are slower, the children become cold much more quickly than others and injuries could result. Clothing must however be suitable for physical activity; it must not interfere with movement nor should there be any danger of it catching on apparatus. This is particularly relevant to children from some ethnic minority groups where there may be problems concerning the removal of jewellery or changing for PE. Bangles and other items worn by both sexes may be religious symbols, and Muslim girls are usually required to cover their arms and legs from a very young age when in mixed company. A teacher needs to be sensitive in explaining to parents the potential hazards of jewellery and flowing clothing during physical activity, particularly when apparatus is involved.

When children with behaviour difficulties are present it is important that lessons are highly structured, well organized and progress smoothly without interruption. Physical environments should have as few distractions as possible; long curtains for instance should be tied back to reduce the temptation to hide behind them! Due consideration also needs to be given to the content of lessons; 'free-flow' or non-stop movement and certain types of accompaniment or stimuli can cause over-excitement and boisterous behaviour. Choice of equipment too should be taken into account, such as a soft ball in games, and the use of the hand rather than a bat may be a necessary precaution. In some instances in gymnastics it may even be wise to limit a child to certain pieces of apparatus which are known to cause least excitement. The teacher needs to keep close to a child with behaviour difficulties and maintain a calm disposition and voice at all times, otherwise the atmosphere to which such children are particularly susceptible can become increasingly tense, thereby exacerbating the situation. Sometimes it is helpful to hold and perhaps hug a child who is being particularly disruptive and a potential danger to others, until equanimity returns. In some dance situations where the dangers are minimal because of the lack of equipment, it may be least disruptive to allow a hyperactive child to continue running around the room for part of the lesson. Other children in the class can very quickly become accustomed to this background 'noise' if attention is not drawn to it, thereby maintaining their own concentration. Teachers also report that while apparently not paying any attention, some hyperactive children are in fact absorbing information.

Class management

Relaxed but effective class management is fundamental not only for safety but also for successful teaching and learning. Many teachers, however, are intimidated by the PE and dance situations, fearing that difficulties encountered in the classroom will be increased when children are encouraged to move freely in large spaces, yet careful preparation and organization can alleviate most problems.

Children with learning or behavioural difficulties respond to clear objectives, structured lessons and materials, and established routines. Conversely problems can arise from a lack of clear direction in a lesson, for children need to know what they are supposed to be doing at all times, from the very start of the lesson. When PE and dance 'lessons' comprise little more than supervised play – the National PE Curriculum permits the teacher a good deal of scope – difficulties are almost certain to arise whether there are children with special needs in the class or not. Materials and teaching approaches can be selected in PE and dance so that all children are involved, working according to their own ability and experiencing success. A change in focus within a lesson can also help maintain attention, perhaps by means of variation in equipment, stimuli, activities and teaching approaches.

There should be established routines in every lesson. Arrangements for changing for PE and dance, moving between the classroom and the hall or playground should follow prescribed patterns; there should be consistent visual and verbal signals which the children can recognize instantly and respond to accordingly. Bringing out and putting away apparatus or equipment provides potential opportunity for disruptive behaviour and it is therefore vital that organization is efficient. Membership of groups should be maintained without change for as long as possible and those with behaviour difficulties placed with more mature children. Everyone should have the experience of working with a range of equipment during a lesson but it is best if each group is given the responsibility of bringing out and putting away certain pieces of apparatus throughout any one term. If possible, apparatus should be placed around the hall (rather than in a cupboard) close to those areas where it will be used by the children, thereby avoiding unnecessary and lengthy carrying of equipment across a room with all the problems this can entail. If the playground or hall is over-large or of an awkward shape the space can be reorganized quickly using clearly recognizable, simple but stable markers so that close visual and aural contact can be maintained with potentially disruptive pupils. On the other hand, children must be given adequate working space because, apart from the obvious physical dangers which could otherwise arise, pupils are more likely to interrupt and aggravate others if in constant close proximity to them. Dramatic weather, imminent festivals or special events can all cause extremes of behaviour and at these times a teacher needs to be particularly alert, selecting materials, planning and organizing in accordance with this possibility.

Recognizing the characteristics of a potentially disruptive situation and therefore diffusing it quietly at an early stage without fuss and without drawing attention to the children concerned is a skill which a teacher must acquire. Simply leading an individual by the hand to a different part of the room as often as necessary while the lesson continues can be very effective. Placing an excitable child near to more mature members of the class can also be helpful. Whenever possible a child's work should be praised and when appropriate his or her ideas employed such as a suggestion for a dance or a game. This is possibly better than asking a child with behavioural problems to demonstrate a skill or movement, as the opportunity to misbehave before a wide audience could prove irresistible and be a destructive experience for everyone concerned.

The teacher's aim should be to maintain a calm and secure working environment for all the children. However a teacher can inadvertently cause confusion and over-excitement by keeping up a constant monologue to no one in particular, as children explore apparatus for instance or by competing with a musical accompaniment in the mistaken belief that this will encourage more imaginative interpretations. Children should be allowed to concentrate on one thing at a time; indeed for many children this is in itself a difficult enough task. Teachers can use periods of general activity to observe the children, noting those who require help and take the opportunity to give attention to those who need it. Long verbal explanations should be avoided, whether addressed to the class as a whole or to particular children; short demonstrations and brief questions, comments and suggestions are more likely to be effective, especially when accompanied by praise and encouragement, in maintaining the interest and concentration of everyone.

Special needs in PE and dance

In order to help all children to take full advantage of the potential offered by participation in PE and dance activities for integrated all-round development a teacher must be aware of the particular needs of individual children. Such knowledge should be used to provide the conditions necessary for learning and to ensure that each child makes progress which is satisfying both to the individual concerned and the teacher. This knowledge however can be misused, as for example when negative preconceptions of the child are formed. Research has frequently demonstrated that children fulfil expectations and, consequently, abilities often remain undeveloped because of lack of opportunity, a hostile environment or an unsympathetic teacher. A physical or sensory impairment, for example, may be viewed as an insurmountable problem rather than regarded in terms of the adaptations necessary on the part of the teacher and the other children in the class. Nor, as indicated at the beginning of this chapter, should it be assumed that a child experiencing specific difficulties in the classroom will automatically have similar problems in PE and dance. It was also demonstrated that a child who is very capable in other areas of the curriculum may be clumsy and uncoordinated in games and gymnastic lessons, causing great personal distress which could well be disregarded by a teacher who does not realize the possible implications for that child's social and emotional development. Teachers therefore not only need relevant background information but should also be alert and responsive to potential difficulties.

Earlier it was pointed out that children with learning difficulties in the classroom can be very gifted physically in terms of agility, strength, co-ordination, grace of movement and skill. Sometimes however there can be problems relating to interpreting visual or verbal information, organizing phrases or sequences, recognizing relationships, and employing simple tactics. Unless a teacher intervenes and helps develop understanding of basic rules and structures, then all-round progress in PE and dance will be limited.

When a child is uncoordinated and clumsy it is vital that every opportunity is taken to increase his or her body awareness and help them acquire basic PE and dance skills during the early years. As well as breaking down material, thereby providing realistic intermediate goals and ensuring that success is a regular experience, time must be allowed for the practice and internalization of skills. If there is the additional difficulty of limited concentration a teacher can help retain attention by the use of intrinsically interesting equipment and stimuli, by working in partnership with the child whenever possible and employing imaginative teaching methods.

Children with emotional problems can be found throughout the intellectual ability range, although the child with learning difficulties and the very gifted are known to be particularly vulnerable. Some children may need PE and dance experiences to release tensions and excess energies, to express feelings, emotions and conflicts. Other children are often withdrawn and so the slightest physical effort must be praised, with the teacher persisting gently until full participation is realized. Experiences which incorporate moments of stillness and movements towards the centre of the body and away from it can be helpful in developing self-awareness and inner equilibrium. Children with emotional difficulties can have problems in establishing relationships with others; PE and dance situations are ideal means of assisting these children make contact with others, a successful relationship with the teacher being the first crucial step.

Confidence, independence and perseverance are often very fragile qualities among children with special needs. Teacher anxieties can easily be conveyed to those with physical or sensory difficulties and so it is important that teachers are themselves confident in knowing as much as possible about each child's capabilities and limitations so that no one is put in a situation which could cause unease. Disabilities should be fully acknowledged as part of the child (with no inhibitions, for instance, in referring to an impairment) and so any necessary modifications to tasks, apparatus arrangements, games and dance structures should be the responsibility, in the first instance, of the teacher but also that of other pupils so that integration can be authentic. Children with disabilities often need to be encouraged to persevere and teachers need to be firm as well as sympathetic in insisting that work is completed properly.

Children with hearing difficulties often try to hide their impairment and so teachers must be alert to this possibility. Incidentally in dance, percussion is a particularly appropriate accompaniment as the vibration can be picked up more easily than other sounds; percussive sounds therefore make effective starting and stopping signals too.

The special needs of children from ethnic minorities, along with many in the indigenous population, are often rooted in poor environmental conditions. Living in high-rise flats with inadequate play areas, for instance, can account for underdeveloped motor co-ordination, low levels of fitness and poor body awareness. Development can also be limited however because of cultural traditions and, in some cases, religious rules. Play learning activities may have a low level of priority in homes which are very disciplined and where imaginative, creative work may not be highly regarded. Immigrant parents, keen for academic success may not realize the value of PE activities in terms of all-round integrated development; playing games for instance may be seen as having little educational value and so children are not encouraged to develop gifts. Teachers must therefore be prepared to explain the importance of participation in PE and dance. Teacher awareness of the traditional sporting preferences and abilities of different groups can also be helpful in involving all children and promoting understanding. Advantage can also be taken of the place dance has in the culture of many ethnic communities, where it is often linked closely with religion or is an integral part of celebrations. Many opportunities arise therefore for the imaginative teacher to involve parents and other members of the local community in providing enriching experiences for all.

Monitoring progress

Throughout this chapter it has been stressed that all children can achieve success and make satisfactory progress in all PE activities. A general enthusiasm for PE is a sure sign that each child is gaining satisfaction from involvement in the planning, performing and evaluating processes. An observant teacher will also find clear indications of a child's physical, motor skill, cognitive, personal and social, aesthetic and creative growth during PE lessons.

For example, improved physical development can be seen in a child who is more alert and whose endurance, fitness, agility, flexibility and mobility have increased. Levels of skill development and general co-ordination can also be clearly observed. Evidence of a child's satisfactory personal and social development may be found in greater involvement and co-operation with other children, sharing equipment, taking turns; sometimes the positive attitudes of other children are signs of social integration. Healthy emotional growth is often first indicated by improved posture, for as self-image improves an upright stance develops replacing the 'hang-dog' look so often found among children who have emotional or learning difficulties. As confidence increases so does independence and with it self-discipline.

Improved cognitive functioning may be shown in PE and dance in the ability to concentrate for progressively longer periods, making appropriate responses to tasks set by the teacher and employing discrimination and selection in the construction of sequences, games and dances. Aesthetic development is shown in a child's grace, sensitivity and harmony of movement; increased awareness of shape and rhythm in personal work and that of others; general interest in and enthusiasm for various sports and dances; the use of aesthetic terms when describing or evaluating. Indicators of creative understanding include the individual nature of responses, imaginative structuring of phrases and sequences, games and dances, and creative interpretations of dance in performance and as a spectator.

The National PE Curriculum subject specific PoS at KS1 and KS2 reproduced in an earlier section of this chapter shows the progress which typically should be expected between the ages of 7 and 11 years within each activity. Clearly the degree of progress will be dependent upon individual special needs, but it is important to note that each child in a class is expected to show improvements in planning, performing, describing and evaluating, in games, gymnastics, dance, swimming, athletics, outdoor and adventurous activities. End of Key Stage Descriptions (EKSDs) describe the types and range of work in PE which most pupils should demonstrate by the end of KS1 and KS2:

Key Stage 1
Pupils plan and perform simple skills safely and show control in linking actions together. They improve their performance through practising their skills, working alone and with a partner. They talk about what they and others have done and are able to make simple judgements. They recognise and experience the changes that happen to their bodies during exercise.

Key Stage 2
Pupils find solutions, sometimes responding imaginatively, to the various challenges they encounter in the different areas of activity. They practise, improve and refine performance, and repeat series of movements they have performed previously, with increasing control and accuracy. They work safely alone, in pairs and in groups, and as members of a team. They make simple judgements about their own and other's performance, and use this information effectively to improve the accuracy, quality and variety of their own performance. They sustain energetic activity over appropriate periods of time, and demonstrate that they understand what is happening to their bodies during exercise.

(DFE, 1995, p. 118)

There are no statutory assessments for PE; the teacher will be relying to a large extent on personal observation skills and these take time and experience to develop. Any checklists should be kept to a minimum, based on the EKSD and be used simply as a reminder to the teacher.

The National Curriculum document suggests that the EKSD are

used to summarize pupils' attainment and form the basis for reporting to parents at the end of the year as well as at the end of a Key Stage. Such reports should be positive, emphasizing what children can do and what they understand, with illustrations from the various activities. Each child's achievements should be indicated along with any involvement in school- and community-based extra-curricular activities. A child's own record (written and visual) of progress or achievement should also be included along with any award gained. The latter could be a badge or a braid awarded for a level of achievement in any activity, swimming for example. Local Education Authorities (LEAs) often have their own awards and so do national bodies such as the RLSS or ASA (Amateur Swimming Association), but perhaps it is more appropriate in primary schools if each school devises its own system so that the stress is on competition with oneself rather than others, and everyone can gain an award. For children with learning difficulties in the classroom, or who have other special needs, the achievement of a badge that can be worn for others to see can have profound positive repercussions.

The availability of a video camera opens up further opportunities. As well as recording performances to show to parents, it is an invaluable aid to developing pupils' evaluations of their own and others' performances, although care must also be taken to avoid misuse of this facility resulting in some children being held up to ridicule. But for those with learning difficulties or emotional problems, where concentration is difficult and memory short, the possibilities are obvious. Some schools may even be fortunate enough to have a still video camera linked to a digitizer. Riley (1993), for example, explains how at the end of a lesson, children with severe learning difficulties are able to see their performances, write about them and print out the sequence of pictures and text for almost immediate recording of achievement.

The rate and extent of progress of each individual, in each of the six activities comprising the National PE Curriculum, and also in terms of planning, performing and describing/evaluating, will be dependent upon a number of factors:

- overall number of children in a class
- proportion of those with special needs in PE
- nature and extent of the special need
- expertise of the teacher in PE
- level of teacher knowledge and understanding of individual SEN
- degree of teaching assistance and other support provided
- availability of appropriate apparatus and equipment.

The National Curriculum however includes a clear commitment to SEN. There is a statutory requirement to make the PE programme available to all children and so teachers should expect the support necessary to fulfil this pledge, including access to appropriate INSET opportunities. In the Further Reading section at the end of this chapter and Useful Addresses at the end of this book information is given on publications and organizations which can offer initial advice and expertise in relation to the whole range of special needs in PE.

Teaching a wide range of SEN in PE is certain to be very challenging, but as numerous teachers point out, it can also be very rewarding not only with reference to the progress that a special needs child can make, but also the way children of all needs and abilities learn to work together and help each other.

REFERENCES

Armstrong, N. (1990) 'Children's physical activity patterns: the implications for physical education'. In *New Directions in Physical Education*, Vol. 1. Leeds: Human Kinetics.

British Association of Advisers and Lecturers in Physical Education (BAALPE) (1989) *Physical Education for Special Educational Needs in Mainstream Education*. Leeds: White Line Press.

Cherrington, D. (1980) *Leverhulme Research Project: Environmental and Motor Deprivation*. Birmingham: Centre of Advisory Studies of Education, University of Birmingham.

Cratty, B.J. (1974) *Motor Activity and the Education of Retardates*. Philadelphia: Lea & Febiger.

Department for Education (DFE) (1995) *Physical Education in the National Curriculum*. London: HMSO.

Frostig, M. and Maslow, P. (1973) *Learning Problems in the Classroom*. New York: Grune & Stratton.

Gordon, N. and McKinley, I. (1980) *Helping Clumsy Children*. London: Churchill Livingstone.

Jowsey, S.E. (1992) *Can I Play too?*. London: David Fulton.

Kephart, N.C. (1960) *The Slow Learner in the Classroom*. Columbus, Ohio: Charles Merrill.

Kitson, V. (1993) Providing opportunities for physical education for children with autism. *The British Journal of Physical Education*, **24** (3) 15.

Knight, E. (1993) Helping pupils with motor co-ordination and associated problems. *The British Journal of Physical Education*, **24** (3) 20–1.

McKinley, I. (1980) 'Rationale for remediation'. In N. Gordon and I. McKinley (eds) *Helping Clumsy Children*. London: Churchill Livingstone.

Morgan, K. and Saunders, J. (1993) Working with special educational needs in a mainstream school – can the end of key stage statement be attained?. *The British Journal of Physical Education*, **24** (3) 16–18.

National Curriculum Council (NCC) (1992) *Physical Education Non-Statutory Guidance*. York.

Riley, S.J. (1993) National Curriculum and assessment of children with severe learning difficulties – a new era?. *The British Journal of Physical Education*, **24** (4) 14–16.

FURTHER READING

Moran, J.M. and Kalakian, L.H. (1978) *Motor Experiences for the Mentally Retarded and Emotionally Disturbed Child*. Minneapolis: Burgess.
Pugh, D. (1993) Teaching physical education to profoundly deaf students in an integrated setting. *The British Journal of Physical Education*, **24** (4) 10–11.
Sanderson, P. (1988) 'Physical education and dance'. In T. Roberts (ed.) *Encouraging Expression: Arts in the Primary Curriculum*. London: Cassell.
Sanderson, P. (1994) 'Unifying the approach to physical education'. In M. Harrison (ed.) *Beyond the Core Curriculum*. Plymouth: Northcote House.

Curriculum materials: special needs

Association of Swimming Therapy (1981) *Swimming for the Disabled*. Wakefield: EP Publishing.
Brown, A. (1987) *Active Games for Children with Movement Problems*. London: Harper & Row.
Kent County Council (nd) *Physical Education; physically handicapped pupils in day schools*. Kent County Council.
Lancashire County Council (1985) *Lancashire Looks at . . . Physical Education in the Special School*. Lancashire County Council.
Levete, G. (1982) *No Handicap to Dance*. London: Souvenir Press.
Price, R.J. (1980) *Physical Education and the Physically Handicapped*. London: Lepus Books.
Russell, J. (1988) *Graded Activities for Children with Motor Difficulties*. Cambridge: Cambridge University Press.
Sherborne, V. (1990) *Developmental movement for children*. Cambridge: Cambridge University Press.
Upton, G. (ed.) (1979) *Physical and Creative Activities for the Mentally Handicapped*. Cambridge: Cambridge University Press.

Curriculum materials: general

There is a wide selection of curriculum literature available on PE and dance in the primary school including that produced by LEAs. Publications from that source which are particularly useful include those of Coventry and of Staffordshire. The relevant addresses are:

City of Coventry
Elm Bank Teacher's Centre
Mile Lane
Coventry CV1 2WN

Staffordshire County Council
PE Section
Education Offices
Tipping Street
Stafford ST16 2DH

Curriculum journals which are well worth consulting include:

The British Journal of Physical Education and also *Primary PE Focus* both published by the Physical Education Association details of which are given in Useful Addresses.

Drama and Dance promoted by Leicester Education Committee, and available from AB Printers Ltd, 33 Cannock Street, Leicester, LE4 7HR.

Dance Matters published by the National Dance Teachers Association, and available from the address given in Useful Addresses.

Arts Education which is the magazine of the National Foundation for Arts Education, may be obtained from Useful Addresses.

All of these publications include invaluable information for the primary school teacher relating to current developments, curriculum materials, forthcoming courses and conferences, relevant resources and so on. SEN in PE and dance are featured regularly.

Audio-visual materials

The achievements of those with special needs can be an inspiration to all teachers and children. Lists of videotapes for sale or hire and suppliers may be found in:

Physical Education and Recreation for People with Special Needs, An Annotated Bibliography (1986). Published by the Physical Education Association.

British Association of Advisers and Lecturers in Physical Education (1989) *Physical Education for Children with Special Educational Needs in Mainstream Education*. Leeds: White Line Press.

Major suppliers of PE and Dance videotapes including SEN are:

Concord Video and Film Council
201 Felixstowe Road
Ipswich IP3 9BJ

DS Information Systems Limited
NAVAL
The Arts Building
Normal College (Top Site)
Siliwen Road
Bangor
Gwynedd LL57 2DZ

Very good tapes of music for dance as well as booklets on dance ideas are produced by:

BBC Educational Publishing
PO Box 234
Wetherby
West Yorkshire LS23 7EU

Research

Journals reporting recent research into various aspects of physical education and dance, and which are readily available include the *Physical Education Review* (from 1995, renamed the *European Physical Education Review*) and the *Research Supplement of The British Journal of Physical Education*.

Useful addresses

ART

NSEAD
(National Society for Education in Art and Design)
7a High Street
Corsham
Wiltshire SN13 0ES

CREATIVE WRITING

Arts Council of Great Britain (Access Unit)
14 Great Peter Street
London SW1P 3NG

Jackson Contra-Banned
Unit 2, Gatehouse Enterprise Centre
Albert Street
Lockwood
Huddersfield HD1 3QD
For mask, puppets and other multicultural resources.

DRAMA

National Drama is the largest UK professional association for teachers, lecturers and theatre workers using drama in educational contexts, including special education. Contact:

National Drama
36 Higher Lane
Upholland
Lancashire WN8 0NL

National Drama also publish, three times a year, *Drama – The Journal of National Drama*, available through membership, or by subscription from:

6 Cornwell Court
Castle Dene
South Gosforth
Newcastle upon Tyne NE3 1TT

Regional associations for teachers using drama exist throughout the country:

CADE (Cheshire Association for Drama in Education)
Cheshire Drama Resource Centre
Verdin Centre
High Street
Winsford CW7 2AY

Drama East
c/o G. Readman
Bishop Grosseteste College
Lincoln

London Drama
Holborn Centre for Performing Arts
Three Cups Yard
Sandland Street
London WC1R 4PZ
(London Drama also run an excellent mail order book service –
Telephone 0171 405 4519)

Norfolk Network For The Teaching of Drama
c/o Norfolk Centre for the Arts in Education
Bull Close Road
Norwich NR3 1NG

Ulster Drama
c/o Stranmillis College
Belfast BT4 5DY

NATE (National Association for the Teaching of English) have a Drama Working Party who organize regional INSET in drama and undertake research. Contact:
NATE
50 Broadfield Road
Broadfield Business Centre
Sheffield S8 0XJ

MUSIC

Nordoff-Robbins Music Centre
2 Lissendon Gardens
London NW5 1PP

Orff-Schulwerk Society
31 Roedean Crescent

London SW15 5JX

British Society for Music Therapy
69 Anondale Avenue
East Barnet
Hertfordshire EN4 8NB
Publishes the *Journal of British Music Therapy*

The Soundbeam Project: enquiries, sales, courses and workshops from:
Tim Swingler
463 Earlham Road
Norwich NR4 7HL

National Music and Disability Information Service
Dartington Hall
Totnes
Devon TQ9 6EJ

Tobin Music
The Old Malthouse
Knight Street
Sawbridgeworth
Hertfordshire CM21 9AX
Colour and music books; publications and courses on the Tobin Music System.

The National Children's Orchestra
157 Craddocks Avenue
Ashtead
Surrey KT21 1NU
There are five orchestras, for talented players aged from 7 to 14 years, which meet during school holidays. Sponsorship and bursary funds are available. Auditions are held in centres throughout the country.

PHYSICAL EDUCATION

If at all possible, individual teachers or schools should join the national associations which can offer much useful advice:

The Physical Education Association
Ling House
5 Western Court
Bromley Street
Birmingham B9 4AN

The National Dance Teachers Association
Treasurer
29 Larkspur Avenue
Walsall
Staffordshire WS7 8SR

The National Foundation for Arts Education
Westminster College
Oxford OX2 9AT

Other organizations which offer very useful advice and information are:

Central Council for Physical Recreation (CCPR)
Francis House
Francis Street
London SW1 1DG

Education Unit
The Arts Council
Piccadilly
London W1
Particularly in relation to the Dance Artists in Schools scheme.

All of the above organizations can supply addresses of the numerous flourishing national and local associations concerned with sport for the disabled where the teacher can seek additional advice and information. However, as far as individual children with special needs are concerned, efforts should be made to integrate them into the local community and so contacts should be made with officials of local community organizations, sports clubs, Cubs, Brownies, leisure centres, swimming baths and dance groups to discover what facilities and arrangements there are for those with special needs. Libraries can usually supply relevant contact names and addresses.

Index